YOU
UNDER THE

MICROSCOPE

YOU
UNDER THE
MICROSCOPE
JENN DLUGOS & CHARLIE HATTON

Cover image credits: ©Adam Linley and Beehive Illustration, and ©Getty Images/Ed Reschke

First published 2023
by Routledge
605 Third Avenue, New York, NY 10158

and by Routledge
4 Park Square, Milton Park, Abingdon, Oxon, OX14 4RN

Routledge is an imprint of the Taylor & Francis Group, an informa business

Library of Congress Cataloging-in-Publication Data
Names: Dlugos, Jenn, author. | Hatton, Charlie, author.
Title: You under the microscope / Jenn Dlugos & Charlie Hatton.
Description: New York, NY : Routledge Press, 2022. | Includes bibliographical references. |
    Audience: Grades 4–6
Identifiers: LCCN 2022003896 (print) | LCCN 2022003897 (ebook) | ISBN 9781032272818 (pbk) |
    ISBN 9781003292111 (ebk)
Subjects: LCSH: Microbiology—Juvenile literature. | Human body—Microbiology—Juvenile literature. |
    Microorganisms—Juvenile literature.
Classification: LCC QR57 .D58 2022 (print) | LCC QR57 (ebook) | DDC 579—dc23/eng/20220525
LC record available at https://lccn.loc.gov/2022003896
LC ebook record available at https://lccn.loc.gov/2022003897

ISBN: 978-1-032-27281-8 (pbk)
ISBN: 978-1-003-29211-1 (ebk)

DOI: 10.4324/9781003292111

Illustrations courtesy of Adam Linley and Beehive Illustration.
Photos courtesy of Shutterstock.
Typeset in Futura PT Condensed
by Raquel Trevino

TABLE OF CONTENTS

INTRODUCTION

If you're reading this book right now, you're probably not doing too many other things. (Although if you happen to be reading this book while singing a sea shanty and hula-hooping atop a unicycle, congratulations—that's some fine multitasking!)

In times of low activity, it can seem like there's nothing much happening, even inside you. If you close your eyes and think about what your body is doing—go ahead; we'll wait—you might feel your heart beating or your breathing, maybe a hungry rumble from your stomach, but that's about it. So there's nothing much else going on in there, right?

Oh, don't you believe it. In fact, your body is a constant swarm of activity—inside, outside, and in every cranny, cell, and capillary between. At a microscopic level, too small to feel or hear or see with the naked eye, every bit inside of you is growing and moving and talking to other bits, morphing into entirely different things, juggling genetic information, fighting tiny battles, working together, keeping watch and pretty much anything else you can think of, short of unicycle-hula hoop shanty singing. (So far as we know.)

Also, notice that we said, "every bit inside of you" rather than "every bit of you". That's because an awful lot of the bits inside of you are not, in fact, you. In addition to the trillions of cells that are you, you (like every other human) play gracious host to even more trillions of hitchhikers along for the ride—from bacteria to viruses to fungi to tiny eight-legged critters that live in your face. (Not, like, "extreme, in your face", but literally inside your face. Yep.)

In this book, you'll learn about some of the amazing feats our organs, our cells, our genes and our "guests" are capable of, many of which are happening right this minute inside all of our bodies—even if we can't see or hear or feel them. Our friend Ana Tomical will help to guide you on the trip, so get ready to take a ride inside (. . . of you)!

I'm your research partner, Ana! Are you ready to take a peek at yourself under the microscope? Ready, set, let's see what you're made of!

GERMS GET UNDER (AND ON) YOUR SKIN

1

Did you wash your hands? You may think your fingers look squeaky clean, but you'd change your mind if you high-fived a Petri dish. Your skin is crawling with germs. Collectively, your colony of skin germs are called your skin flora.

Petri dishes contain agar, which comes from algae. Agar is rich with nutrients that allow bacteria, fungi, and other microbes to grow.

The germs on your skin's surface are called transient skin flora. Your transient skin flora changes based on the surfaces you touch. These germs are removed by handwashing.

Skin surface

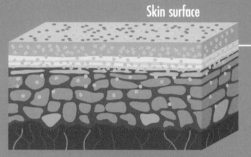

○ Transient flora
● Resident flora

Resident skin flora are microbes that live in the deep layers of the skin. Many of these microbes help to protect your body from infection. These germs cannot be removed by handwashing.

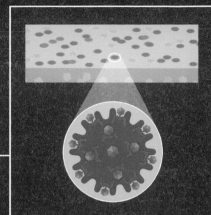

Your transient flora can include viruses, like the flu virus. You can pick up this virus by touching a surface that an infected person touched. Washing your hands will help to kill these harmful germs and help to prevent you from getting sick.

If you press your fingers into a Petri dish, some of the microbes from your skin will transfer to the agar and start to grow. The different colors and patterns represent different colonies of fungi and bacteria on your skin's surface.

COMMON MISSED AREAS OF HANDWASHING

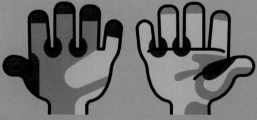

■ Areas most frequently missed   ■ Not missed
■ Areas less frequently missed

Wash your hands thoroughly. A good rule of thumb is to sing Happy Birthday twice while washing. Or quietly hum your favorite boy band song. (We know you have one, and no one will hear you over the water running anyway.)

"Who says you can't listen to your favorite boy band sing Happy Birthday while you wash?"

DOI: 10.4324/9781003292111-1

1

GERMOPOLIS

You've got cooties. Yes, you. And so do your friends, family, and everyone you know. The human body is home to many different types of bacteria, fungi, and other microbes. Before you get too grossed out, many of these microbes are beneficial to you, and some are crucial to your survival. So, let's take a tour through your own Germopolis.

GERM CENSUS

Scientists once believed that the bacteria inside the human body outnumbered human cells by 10 to 1. However, the actual estimate might be closer to 1 to 1.3 bacteria for every human cell. Considering that there are about 37 trillion cells in the human body, that is still trillions of microbes living inside of you! These microbes are much smaller than human cells. Therefore, these trillions of microbes take up a very small portion of your body mass.

DIVERSITY IS THE SPICE OF (YOUR) LIFE

Your personal Germopolis contains many different residents, such as:

Prokaryotes (cells that have no nucleus)	Eukaryotes (cells with a nucleus)	Viruses (have no cells, infect other cells)

DOI: 10.4324/9781003292111-2

"WHO NOSE THERE?"

The microbes in your nose help develop your nose tissues, and some microbes may even affect how well you smell. A recent study found that people who had butyric acid-producing bacteria (a common type of gut bacteria) in their nose had a worse sense of smell than people who did not.

RESIDENT GERMS MUST SHOW ID

Just like your fingerprints, the combination of germs that live inside your body is unique to you. You receive some microbes from your mother before and during birth. The rest come from your interactions with the environment. Even identical twins develop different combinations of microbes.

Have your Germ I.D. ready!

THE HOT SPOT IN TOWN

Your largest bacterial colony is inside your digestive tract. Between 300 and 500 species of bacteria live in your digestive tract.

GROWING PAINS FOR MICROBES

Your Germopolis did not become stable until you were 2 or 3 years old. This likely happens because infants go through a lot of changes in the first years of life, which causes the microbe populations within their bodies to change drastically, too.

COLON CAFÉ

3 MANY MORE MICROBIOMES

While the digestive tract, or "gut," biome gets a lot of attention—and rightfully so; we wouldn't enjoy ice cream very much without it!—it's not the only bacterial boomtown boosting your body. We've got biomes oozing all over us. Here are just a few:

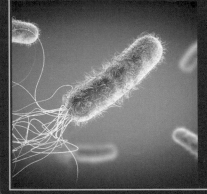

EYE MICROBIOME

You wouldn't want most bacteria and viruses in your eyes, but a few particular species may help keep us healthy. Our eyes contain only about 1/100th the number of bacteria on skin. (Though contact lens wearers tend to have more bacteria, and more species.) But those present may help our bodies repel other bacteria that cause dry eyes, blindness and other conditions.

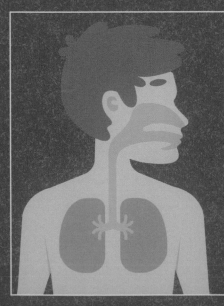

LUNG MICROBIOME

Healthy lungs were long thought to be free of outside organisms, but scientists have found more than one hundred different species of bacteria in the lungs of healthy subjects. These bacteria ride down from the mouth in small numbers and make themselves at home in our lungs, possibly helping our bodies to control inflammation and prevent disease-causing infections.

DOI: 10.4324/9781003292111-3

NASAL MICROBIOME

If the eyes have it, the nose knows, too! As you might expect by now, we all indeed have thriving colonies of bacteria living up our schnozzes. A 2020 study suggests that at least one species may have adapted specifically to living "la vida nose-a". Other research suggests that the specific bacteria in each of our snouts may reflect—or impact—the types of smells we detect.

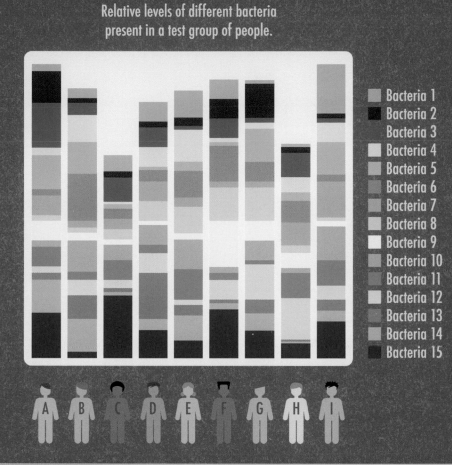

Relative levels of different bacteria present in a test group of people.

Bacteria 1
Bacteria 2
Bacteria 3
Bacteria 4
Bacteria 5
Bacteria 6
Bacteria 7
Bacteria 8
Bacteria 9
Bacteria 10
Bacteria 11
Bacteria 12
Bacteria 13
Bacteria 14
Bacteria 15

A B C D E F G H I

NAVEL MICROBIOME

Though technically part of your skin, the relative isolation of the navel microbiome has made it an interesting area for scientists to dive "innie" to. (Sorry.) One study of 60 volunteers' belly button bacteria found over 2,000 unique species, but six were found in more than 80% of subjects—a species diversity pattern similar to trees in a rain forest. Far outie! (Again, so sorry.)

So, is it still safe to wash behind my ears?

IT TAKES GUTS TO BE THIS GERMY

Your digestive tract is packed with germs—approximately 300 to 500 different types of germs, in fact! And, trust us, you wouldn't want it any other way. Here are some benefits that these germy gut residents provide.

Your gut bacteria help to digest foods that your body cannot digest, such as the sugars in dairy products and fiber and other carbohydrates from plants.

A way to a person's heart is through their...gut bacteria? Scientists have found that people who have heart disease have different gut bacteria compared to people who do not. More research into this difference could lead to new methods to treat or prevent heart disease.

Your gut bacteria contain a mix of beneficial and harmful germs. In a healthy gut, the good germs keep the bad germs in check, so the "baddies" don't multiply and make you sick.

Gut bacteria help your body to produce vitamin K. Vitamin K helps with blood clotting, which is important for wound healing. In fact, your gut bacteria produce about half of the vitamin K you need per day.

6

DOI: 10.4324/9781003292111-4

BALANCING YOUR GUT BACTERIA LIKE A PRO (OR A PRE!)

Many factors affect your gut bacteria. Some you can control, while others you cannot. Let's take a closer look at factors that affect your gut bacteria.

Your gut bacteria changes with age. By age 60, people tend to have fewer species of bacteria. Bacteria that help with digestion tend to decrease in number.

No. of gut bacteria species

0   30   60
Age

The types of foods you eat may affect gut bacteria. Foods that go through fermentation—called fermented foods—contain probiotics. Probiotics are beneficial bacteria that may help to balance gut bacteria in some people.

pro biotic Kefir

Yogurt

probiotic Kombucha

live bacteria Sauerkraut

Since probiotic foods contain live bacteria, people who have weak immune systems or certain chronic diseases should not eat probiotics before talking to their doctor.

Taking certain medications can affect gut bacteria. For example, taking antibiotics to treat bacterial infections can temporarily affect your balance of gut bacteria.

BRAN BOWL

Your gut bacteria eat some types of fiber that your digestive system cannot digest. Prebiotic foods are foods that are rich in this type of fiber. Fruits, vegetables, and whole grains are sources of prebiotics.

There are no official dietary recommendations for probiotic and prebiotic foods. Instead, you can keep your gut bacteria healthy by:
- eating a well-balanced diet
- following your doctor's instructions when taking antibiotics and other medications
- being physically active, whenever possible
- talking to your doctor if you have digestive problems.

DOI: 10.4324/9781003292111-5

7

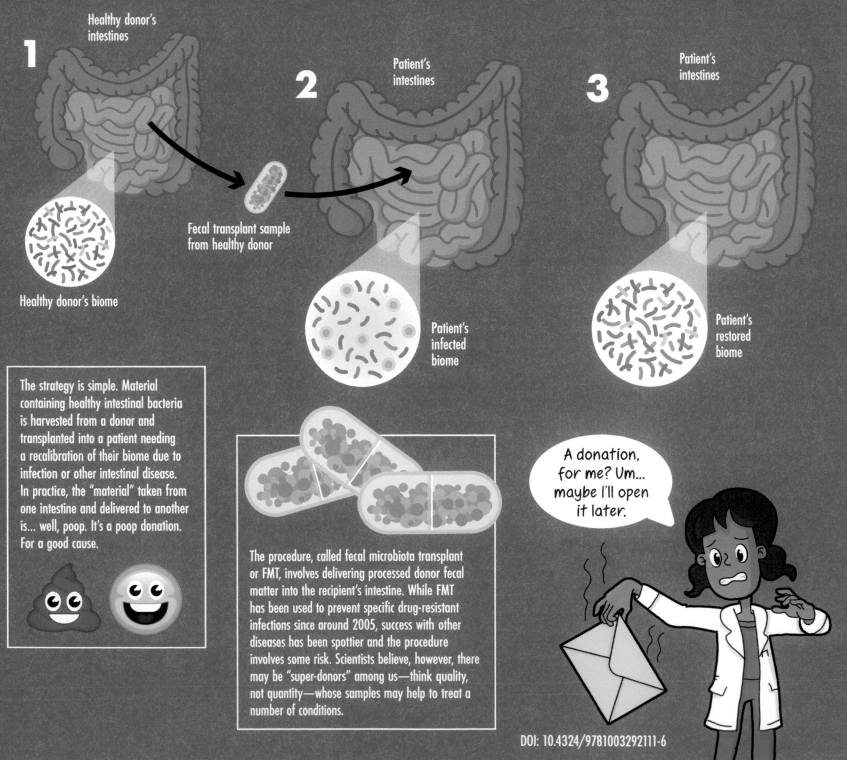

6 BRING BACK MY BIOME TO ME

You've read about the importance of a healthy gut microbiome. But what can you do if your gut biome *isn't* so healthy, due to imbalance or aggressive antibiotic treatment? In extreme cases, you can try borrowing someone else's.

1 Healthy donor's intestines

Healthy donor's biome

Fecal transplant sample from healthy donor

2 Patient's intestines

Patient's infected biome

3 Patient's intestines

Patient's restored biome

The strategy is simple. Material containing healthy intestinal bacteria is harvested from a donor and transplanted into a patient needing a recalibration of their biome due to infection or other intestinal disease. In practice, the "material" taken from one intestine and delivered to another is... well, poop. It's a poop donation. For a good cause.

The procedure, called fecal microbiota transplant or FMT, involves delivering processed donor fecal matter into the recipient's intestine. While FMT has been used to prevent specific drug-resistant infections since around 2005, success with other diseases has been spottier and the procedure involves some risk. Scientists believe, however, there may be "super-donors" among us—think quality, not quantity—whose samples may help to treat a number of conditions.

A donation, for me? Um... maybe I'll open it later.

DOI: 10.4324/9781003292111-6

LET'S HAVE SOME FUN(GI)

In the human microbiome, bacteria have gotten most of the research attention—but they're not the only hitchhikers taking us for a ride. Several species of microscopic fungus live on and inside us, too. And not just the kind that cause athlete's foot. (But possibly those, too.) Follow on for fun facts focused on our fungal friends.

Just as with our stowaway bacteria, we have many different "mycobiomes", or populations of fungus (*myco-* means "fungus") living in different parts of our body. The particular species present and the amount of each can be very different from body site to body site, or—even at the same site—from person to person.

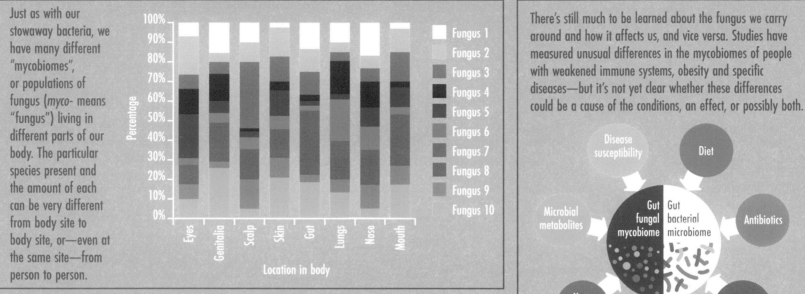

There's still much to be learned about the fungus we carry around and how it affects us, and vice versa. Studies have measured unusual differences in the mycobiomes of people with weakened immune systems, obesity and specific diseases—but it's not yet clear whether these differences could be a cause of the conditions, an effect, or possibly both.

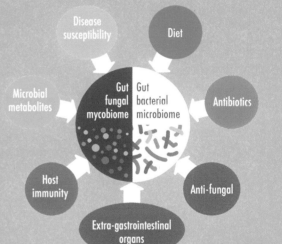

Researchers have found fungus species in the mouths, digestive tracts and on the skin of infants and newborns. While the types present typically overlap with species passed from their mothers through contact and milk, the young tykes' fungi aren't all hand-me-downs. Scientists are researching the additional factors that influence how our mycobiomes develop.

As long as you're not a mushroom, you're perfectly welcome.

DOI: 10.4324/9781003292111-7

9

MITE YOU SPARE A FOLLICLE?

Ah. A nice relaxing afternoon with just you and thousands of microscopic arachnids. We hate to break it to you, but right now you have tiny mites crawling all over your face. The good news is that these mites do not bother most people, and they actually have some fascinating characteristics (once you get over the fact that these creepy spider relatives consider your face their home).

Scientists look for mites by doing face scrapings. They use a tool to gently scrape the surface of a person's cheek, and then look at the sample under the microscope. A recent study found that actual mites only appeared on 10–14 percent of the face scrapings, however every sample had mite DNA. That means that mites were in the skin, even if the mites themselves dodged the face scrape.

The scientific name for skin mites is *Demodex*. *Demodex* live on the skin of most mammals, including humans. These mites are host-specific, which means that the type of *Demodex* mites that live on your furry pets are different from the type that live on you.

Scientists have found skin mites living on every mammal, except for members of the platypus family. The platypus is one of the very few mammals that lay eggs, so they are pretty content with being the weirdos of the mammals.

For most people, face mites do not cause any noticeable health issue and do not have to be treated. They may be gross to think about, but face mites are a normal part of being human.

NEW!
Mite-be-gone

10

DOI: 10.4324/9781003292111-8

Human face mites in Asian countries have different gene mutations than those in European or African countries. This finding can help scientists track how humans and our tiny face friends evolved over time.

There are two types of mites that live on your face. Everyone has these mites, but scientists are not quite sure how they started living on us in the first place. Early humans most likely got these microscopic freeloaders from our ape ancestors.

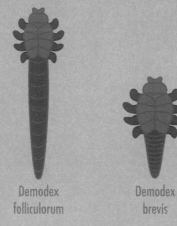

Demodex folliculorum

Demodex brevis

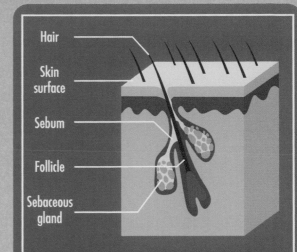

Hair

Skin surface

Sebum

Follicle

Sebaceous gland

Most of the mites living on your skin hang out on your face, probably because facial skin has large pores and a lot of sebaceous (pronounced suh-BAY-shuss) glands. Sebaceous glands secrete sebum, an oily substance that keeps the skin moist, reduces friction, and makes your skin waterproof. The mites eat skin cells, sebum, and hormones produced by your body.

In a small percentage of people, *Demodex* mites can contribute to certain skin conditions. For example, some cases of rosacea (pronounced ro-ZAY-shuh) may be caused when a person has a reaction to bacteria carried by the mites. Fortunately, rosacea can be treated with antibiotics and medicated skin creams.

Apply to skin twice a day to reduce redness.

Call your dermatologist if you have any questions.

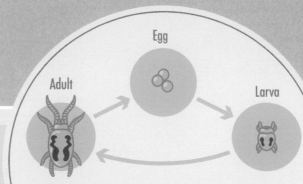

Egg

Adult

Larva

The life cycle of face mites from birth to reproduction is only 14 days. The mites lay their eggs in the hair follicles or sebaceous glands. When the eggs hatch, they only spend a week in the larvae stage before they become adults. On day 14, the adults lay eggs. Adults only live a few weeks.

Does the thought of a dusty room make you want to sneeze? The culprit may just be microscopic dust mites living in your house. Let's take a closer look at these dust-loving bugs, and what you can do to control the ah-choos.

Dust is a solid waste material. The composition of dust in your home can differ depending on your behavior. For example, you can bring in dirt and pollen from outside that becomes part of your dust.

COMPONENTS OF DUST

Dust mites	Live and dead insects	Human and pet skin cells	Hair	Clothing fibers	Bacteria	Soil	Pollen

Dust mites are microscopic arachnids that live in house dust, beds, curtains, stuffed animals, and carpets. They eat dead skin cells sloughed off by humans and pets.

WHAT CAUSES ALLERGIES?

Dust allergies are an allergic reaction to the waste produced by dust mites.

1. Foreign substance enters the body.

2. Immune system has strong reaction to the substance.

3. Antibodies are produced.

4. Antibodies attach to cells. Cells produce chemicals that increase inflammation and mucous production. You feel sneezy and congested.

Dust mite allergies can be difficult to diagnose because allergies to pollen, pets, and other substances also cause similar symptoms. Doctors can do tests to determine what type of allergies a person has.

DOI: 10.4324/9781003292111-9

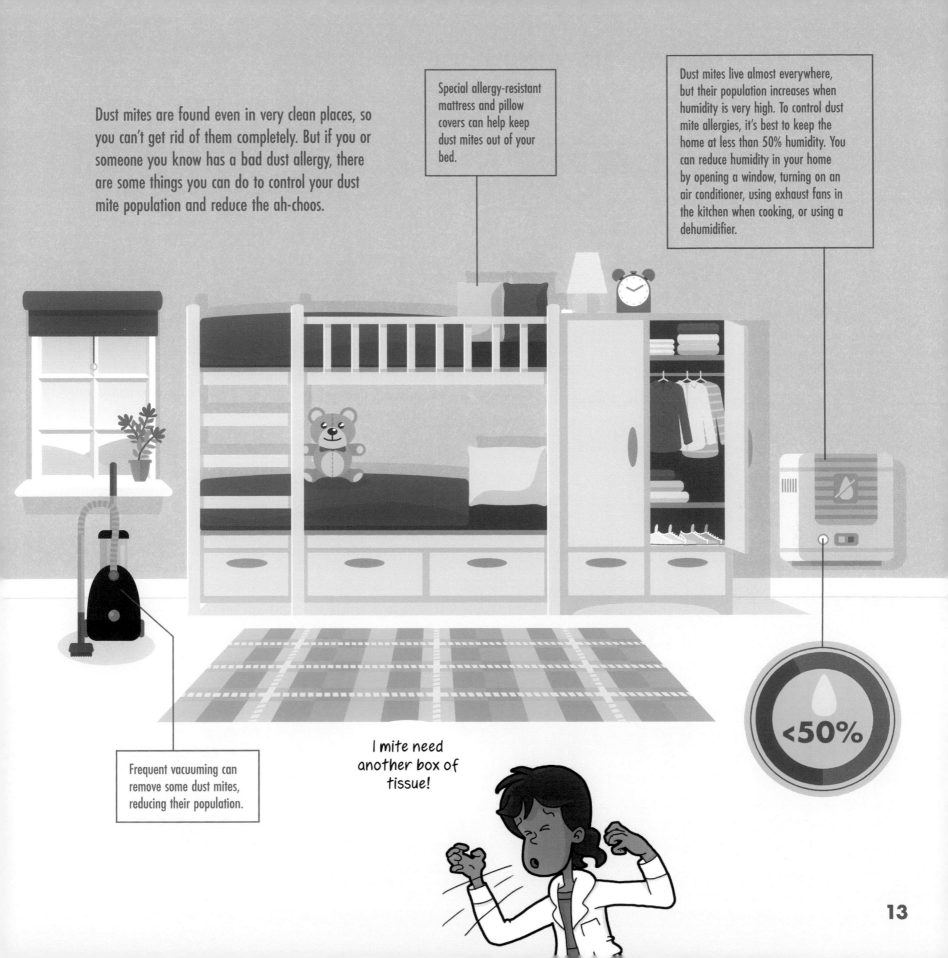

Dust mites are found even in very clean places, so you can't get rid of them completely. But if you or someone you know has a bad dust allergy, there are some things you can do to control your dust mite population and reduce the ah-choos.

Special allergy-resistant mattress and pillow covers can help keep dust mites out of your bed.

Dust mites live almost everywhere, but their population increases when humidity is very high. To control dust mite allergies, it's best to keep the home at less than 50% humidity. You can reduce humidity in your home by opening a window, turning on an air conditioner, using exhaust fans in the kitchen when cooking, or using a dehumidifier.

Frequent vacuuming can remove some dust mites, reducing their population.

I mite need another box of tissue!

<50%

10 BEDS, BUGS AND BEYOND

You can make the case that many of the critters hitching a ride on (or in) our bodies are useful. Some bacteria are harmful—but others are important for our health and survival. Viruses can make us sick—but may also play an important role in our genetics. You might think there's no case to be made for pests like lice and bedbugs. And you'd mostly be right. But only *mostly*.

Let's get the unpleasantries out of the way. Lice and bedbugs are parasitic insects that survive by climbing onto warm-blooded animals, biting down and sucking blood. While these blood-binging bullies bother many animal species, some populations—three types of lice and a distinct subset of bedbugs—set their sinister sights specifically on humans. Oh, goody.

Clearly, finding lice or bedbugs on or around us would tell us something about our future. (Namely, that we'll probably be meeting an exterminator soon.) And it would tell us something about our present. (That it's time to call that exterminator.) But can these irritating insects tell us anything about our past? Yes, they can—millions of years of it, in fact.

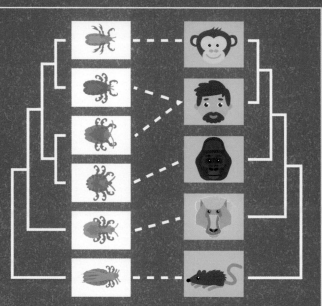

By comparing differences in the DNA of different bedbug species, scientists estimate the pests have been around for at least 100 million years, meaning they coexisted with—but probably didn't chomp on—dinosaurs. It's thought that humans first attracted bedbug attention when early humans sought shelter in caves full of birds or bats—long-time and favorite bedbug hosts.

EVOLUTION OF BEDBUGS SPECIES

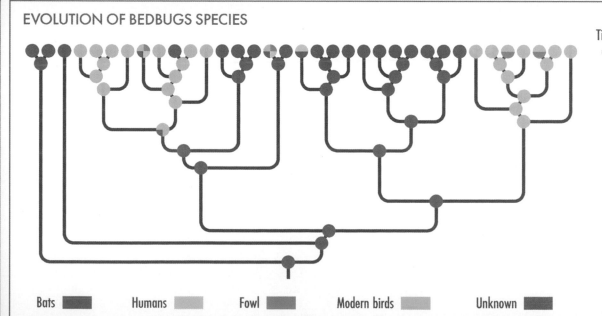

Bats | Humans | Fowl | Modern birds | Unknown

Time

Digging deeper into bedbug genomes—which seems only fair—researchers measured differences among members of a single species, some that harangue humans and others that bother bats. Based on the degree of difference, they estimate that humans moved out of caves around 250,000 years ago for other shelters, taking their new bedbug "friends" along with them.

14

DOI: 10.4324/9781003292111-10

Over thousands of years, the bedbugs living on humans developed different characteristics, with each bedbug population becoming more suited to its more convenient host. Both bugs can still be a bother, though—when bats get into houses, their "bat bugs" have been known to bite humans in a pinch. Any blood supply will do in an emergency, we suppose.

BED BUG — Short fringe hairs

BAT BUG — Long fringe hairs

If bedbugs blew your mind, get a load of lice. Three species of lice infest humans, living on different parts of the body—and they each tell us something about our past. One type of human louse is closely related to a species that today infests gorillas, and scientists believe our ancestors picked it up from encounters with large ancient apes 3—4 million years ago.

Another species of louse appears to have evolved on Neanderthals, now-extinct close relatives of humans. Most humans carry a small percentage of Neanderthal DNA, so perhaps it's only natural that our species also inherited their lice, starting around 60,000 years ago.

The last louse species making hosts of humans lives in clothing, and likely developed from the species that lives among hair on the head. Genetic differences between the species suggest that they diverged between around 80,000 to 170,000 years ago—which also suggests that's the time that early humans started regularly making and wearing layers of clothes.

Why does learning history make me so...*itchy?*

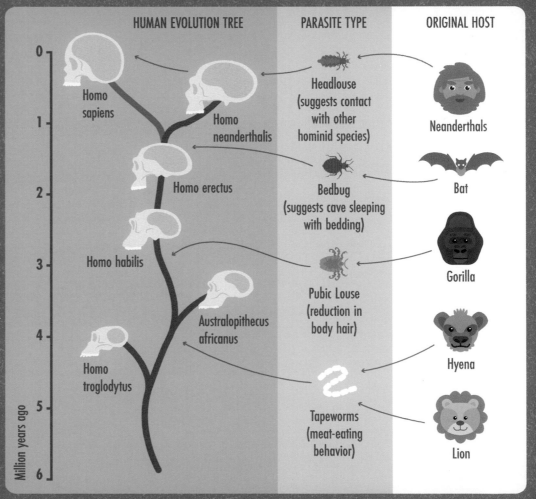

INCREDIBLY CRAFTY CRITTERS

You've got to hand it to parasites. (Actually, no, you really don't have to hand it to parasites. But hear us out here.) Parasites make a whole living out of latching onto humans, scarfing food and warmth and shelter, all without lifting a proboscis to help us. One parasitic species may even be able to control our minds. Impressive—even if it's probably accidental.

The parasite in question is *Toxoplasma gondii*, a protozoan (pro-tuh-ZOH-an, a single-celled eukaryote) that infects warm-blooded animals—including humans, where it usually causes mild or no symptoms—but can only reproduce in the digestive tracts of cats. How does a lonely protozoan stuck in, say, a rat get itself back into a cat? That's where the mind control comes in.

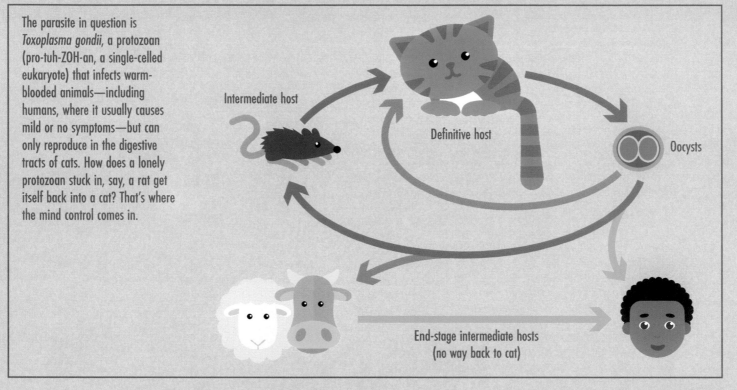

Intermediate host

Definitive host

Oocysts

End-stage intermediate hosts
(no way back to cat)

Rats and mice usually run away when they smell cat urine, for reasons Tom & Jerry and Itchy & Scratchy make all too clear. But rodents infected with *Toxoplasma gondii* don't run away from cat pee—they run *toward* it, instead. The parasite, which very much wants the cat to eat its unsuspecting host, releases a signal that completely changes host behavior—for the worse.

Where do we come in? *Toxoplasma* is estimated to infect around two billion people. Scientists have tested whether certain disorders may be linked with infection, with mixed results—but one test was clear: when asked about the "pleasantness" of cat urine odor, infected men (more) and women (less) rated it significantly differently than did uninfected people. Me-yow?

No comment. Ew.

DOI: 10.4324/9781003292111-11

I SPY, INSIDE MY LITTLE EYE...

To see most of the microscopic things discussed in this book, you'd need... well, a microscope. We may have given the answer away in the book title, frankly. But there may be one otherwise-undetectable-by-the-naked-eye phenomenon that you *can* see without additional equipment—if you happen to have vitreous floaters.

Vitreous floaters, or "eye floaters", dance around and across many peoples' fields of vision—perhaps more than 75% of the population, according to some studies. Floaters may appear as spots, fuzzy lines or "cobwebs" that float (hence the name!) across the visual field and typically slide away if you try to focus on them directly.

"They're fascinating and aggravating, all at the same time!"

In most people, floaters are caused by material floating in the vitreous humor, the large chamber of the eye behind the lens. The vitreous humor is mostly water, but it contains strands of collagen that give it the texture of a squishy gel. (If it sounds like Jell-O, yeah—it's basically raw Jell-O.) Over time, the collagen or cell debris can clump together and become visible.

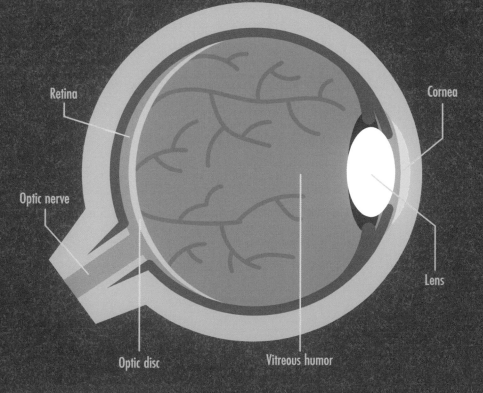

Retina

Cornea

Optic nerve

Optic disc

Vitreous humor

Lens

VITREOUS COLLAGEN FIBER

Most floaters are harmless—if annoying—though a large number or sudden appearance could be a sign of a serious condition. They're also more common in near- and far-sighted and older people. But here's a thing: vitreous collagen fibers are tiny, around 30 nanometers wide. Even clumped together, it's unlikely you could see them if they weren't right inside your eyes.

DOI: 10.4324/9781003292111-12

13 MICROBES TO THE RESCUE!

You already know that there are beneficial microbes, but some microbes take their goodness to Little Miss Goody-Good levels. In fact, some microbes are so good, they can nurse you back to health when you are sick, or prevent you from getting sick in the first place.

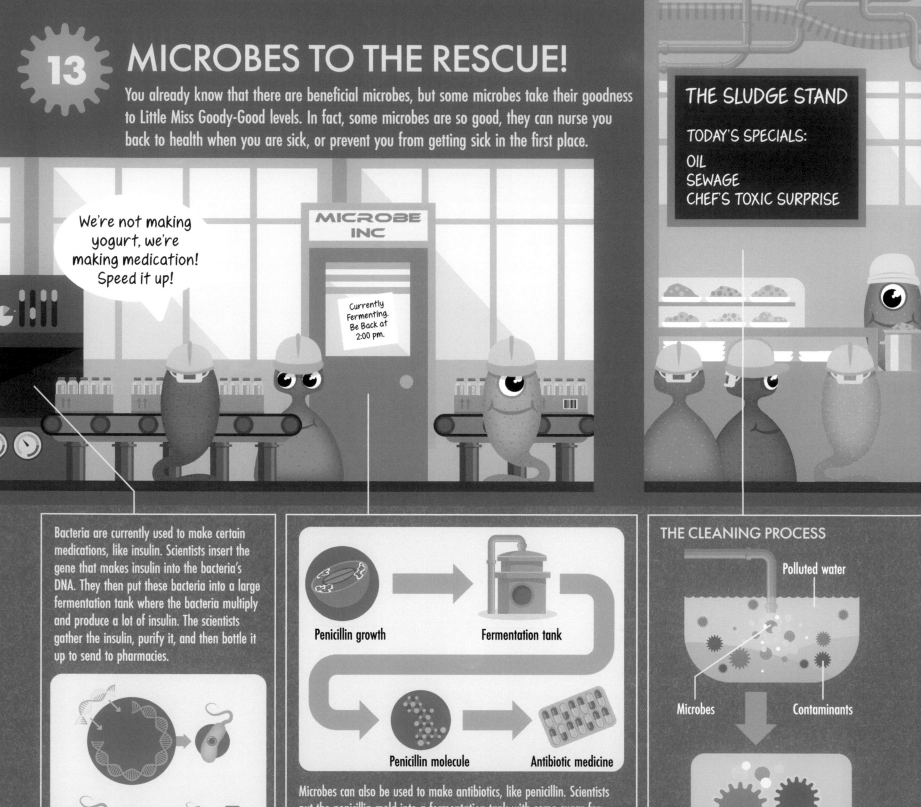

THE SLUDGE STAND

TODAY'S SPECIALS:

OIL
SEWAGE
CHEF'S TOXIC SURPRISE

We're not making yogurt, we're making medication! Speed it up!

MICROBE INC

Currently Fermenting. Be Back at 2:00 pm.

Bacteria are currently used to make certain medications, like insulin. Scientists insert the gene that makes insulin into the bacteria's DNA. They then put these bacteria into a large fermentation tank where the bacteria multiply and produce a lot of insulin. The scientists gather the insulin, purify it, and then bottle it up to send to pharmacies.

Penicillin growth → Fermentation tank

Penicillin molecule → Antibiotic medicine

Microbes can also be used to make antibiotics, like penicillin. Scientists put the penicillin mold into a fermentation tank with some sugar for food (yes, fungi have a sweet tooth. Or they would if they actually had teeth.). Inside the tank, the fungi produce the penicillin that is then purified, packaged, and used to treat bacterial infections.

THE CLEANING PROCESS

Polluted water

Microbes   Contaminants

Microbes digest contaminants

DOI: 10.4324/9781003292111-13

If you have ever had a *Salmonella* infection from eating uncooked or spoiled food, you're probably never going to forget it (and neither is your bathroom). As unpleasant as *Salmonella* is to your digestive system, these bacteria seem to be even more infectious to cancer cells. Scientists are trying to genetically modify *Salmonella* bacteria to be an effective and safe treatment for cancers.

SHIPPING CENTER →

Salmonella Collection

Some types of bacteria are also used to clean up oil spills, remove pollutants from soils and lakes, and even clean wastewater. This helps to keep the water you drink, swim in, and load into your squirt-gun clean and safe (well, safe for anyone who is NOT on the receiving end of your squirt-gun, that is).

MICROBE INC

KEEPING HUMANS HEALTHY ONE MICROBE AT A TIME

Scientists are currently trying to use bacteria to build tiny microbots that can deliver medicine directly into human body cells. They are even looking into using magnetic bacteria, which can be guided to the correct part of the body using a magnet outside of the body.

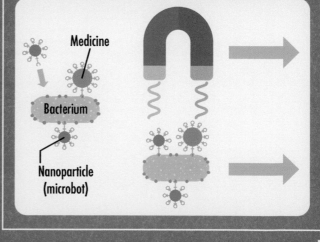

Medicine

Bacterium

Nanoparticle (microbot)

14 WE ALL GO VIRAL

If your brain boggles at the thought of 38 trillion bacteria (give or take a few billion) riding you around the planet, we hope this won't break your boggler completely: you're also stuffed full of viruses—380 trillion of them, in fact. That's one heck of a party you're throwing.

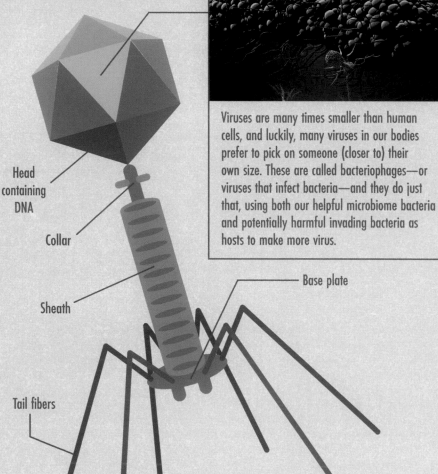

Head containing DNA

Collar

Sheath

Base plate

Tail fibers

Viruses are many times smaller than human cells, and luckily, many viruses in our bodies prefer to pick on someone (closer to) their own size. These are called bacteriophages—or viruses that infect bacteria—and they do just that, using both our helpful microbiome bacteria and potentially harmful invading bacteria as hosts to make more virus.

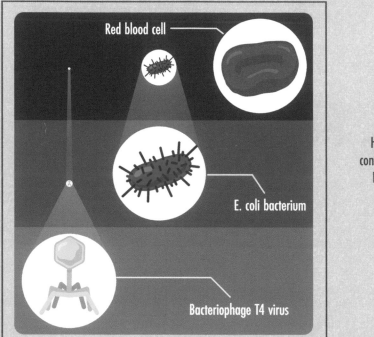

Red blood cell

E. coli bacterium

Bacteriophage T4 virus

The good news—if there's any "good news" about every cell in your body being outnumbered ten to one by viruses—is that (a) viruses aren't very big, and (b) many of them aren't actually interested in us. Most viruses are 100 nanometers wide or so. (A nanometer [or nm] is one-billionth of a meter, and 100 nm is about one-thousandth the width of a human hair.)

Scientists are just beginning to learn about our "human virome"—studies have found that the types of viruses in our intestines can be very different from person to person, but don't tend to change much in each individual over time. On the other hand, people who live together tend to share many of the same viruses, as they're passed back and forth in the close environment.

DOI: 10.4324/9781003292111-14

So there's a vast army of viruses pulsing through our bodies, but they may be helping a little or hurting a little or busy infecting bacteria, so it's fine, right? We're sure it's fine. Oh, did we mention the countless viruses that have burrowed into our genomes over millions of years, so that our DNA is possibly more virus than human at this point? We should talk about that.

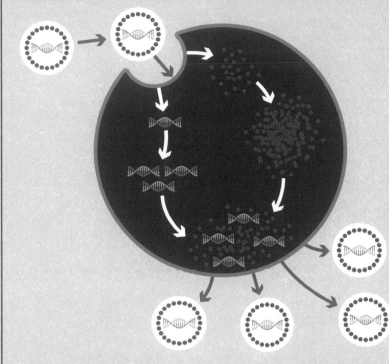

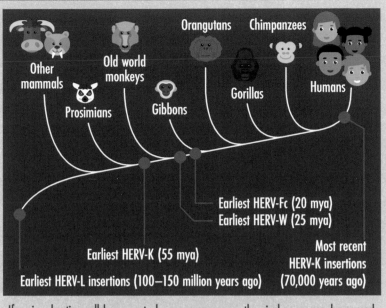

Whether viruses are invading bacteria, plant cells or—well, *us*—they usually enter cells, hijack the cellular machinery to make many viral copies, then send the copies out to repeat the process. In some cases, this kills the "host" cell. In others, though, the virus inserts its genetic material into the host's genome, so it gets copied and passed on when the cell divides.

If a virus-hosting cell happens to be a sperm or egg, the viral genes can be passed to future generations. Viruses called HERVs insert genes between sequences known as LTRs, or long terminal repeats. By searching for LTRs, we see evidence of HERVs inserted into our ancestors' DNA more than 100 million years ago, and about 8% of our DNA is HERV-related.

Most HERVs and other human genome viruses have mutated over time and can no longer activate—or possibly be recognized as viruses. At least 45% of our human genome appears to be associated with inserted viruses, but it could be as high as 70%. Some inserted viruses have altered the way neighboring genes behave, permanently affecting the path of human evolution.

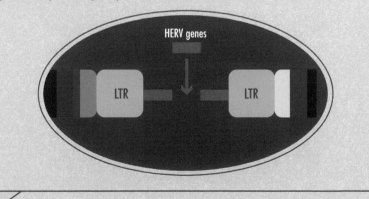

I thought I was at least 45% sugar and spice?

HUMAN CHROMOSOME SEQUENCE

IF YOU CAN'T BEAT 'EM...

Mitochondria

Strand of DNA

Nucleus (contains DNA)

All the cells in your body—and those in nearly all plants and animals, from lions to dandelions, from lima beans to Mr. Bean—keep their innards neat and tidy. Each of our cells wrap their DNA in a package called a nucleus, and contain other "organelles", or wrapped-up cellular compartments, to produce energy, form proteins and perform other important functions.

But not every type of cell cleans its room and makes its bed. Unlike nucleus-containing cells, or eukaryotes, cells called prokaryotes don't have nuclei. These cells, which include bacteria, let their DNA float free. In fact, prokaryotes don't have any organelles. Their stuff is just flung all over, like a tornado hit the place.

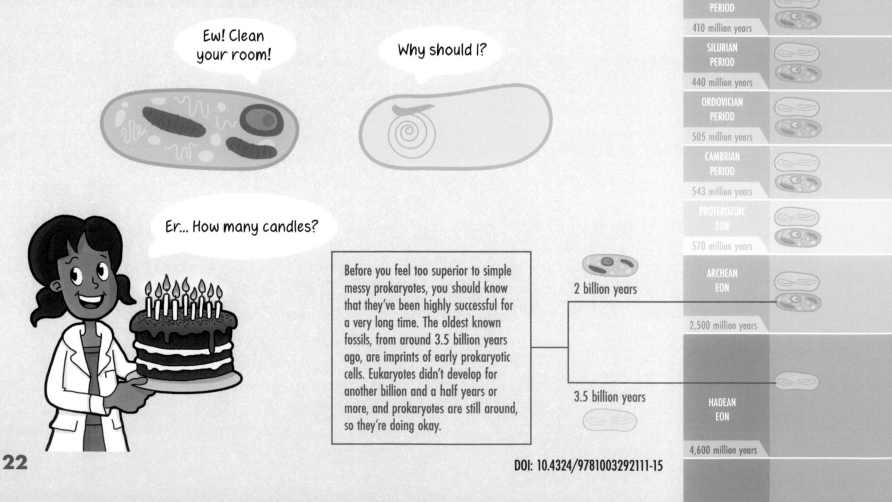

Ew! Clean your room!

Why should I?

Er... How many candles?

Before you feel too superior to simple messy prokaryotes, you should know that they've been highly successful for a very long time. The oldest known fossils, from around 3.5 billion years ago, are imprints of early prokaryotic cells. Eukaryotes didn't develop for another billion and a half years or more, and prokaryotes are still around, so they're doing okay.

2 billion years

3.5 billion years

QUATERNARY PERIOD
1.8 million years

TERTIARY PERIOD
50 million years

CRETACEOUS PERIOD
148 million years

JURASSIC PERIOD
208 million years

TRIASSIC PERIOD
245 million years

PERMIAN PERIOD
286 million years

CARBONIFEROUS PERIOD
360 million years

DEVONIAN PERIOD
410 million years

SILURIAN PERIOD
440 million years

ORDOVICIAN PERIOD
505 million years

CAMBRIAN PERIOD
543 million years

PROTEROZOIC EON
570 million years

2,500 million years

ARCHEAN EON

HADEAN EON

4,600 million years

DOI: 10.4324/9781003292111-15

...SWALLOW 'EM WHOLE

The question is: how did eukaryotes manage to collect all their stuff? The answer: no one knows for sure. (We don't have a lot of TikToks from two billion years ago to explain what organisms were doing at the time.)

So far, most evidence points to a process called "endosymbiosis" (IN-dough-SIM-bee-oh-sis). You may have heard of "symbiosis", where two species cooperate to benefit both, like bees spreading flower pollen while they gather nectar, or your dog eating your delicious unfinished homework. The "endo" bit means one of those organisms lives inside the other, like this:

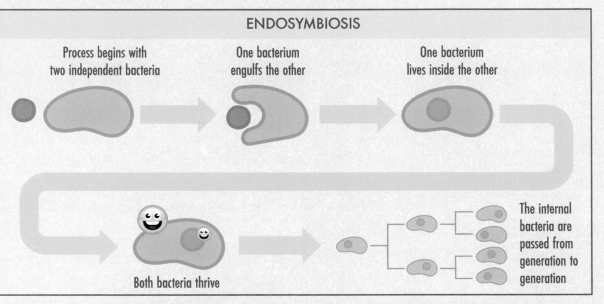

ENDOSYMBIOSIS

Process begins with two independent bacteria

One bacterium engulfs the other

One bacterium lives inside the other

Both bacteria thrive

The internal bacteria are passed from generation to generation

In this case, the "inner" prokaryote might benefit from protection against other cells that want to eat it. In turn, that cell may provide the "outer" one with something it's lacking, like making nutrients or converting sunlight to energy or a cool music collection. If the internal cells can be passed on when the outer one splits, this friendly arrangement can continue for millennia.

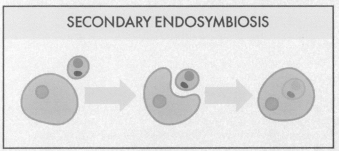

SECONDARY ENDOSYMBIOSIS

Have you ever thought about charging rent?

This process, or something similar, may have happened many times, eventually forming eukaryotes—and many, many types of those—from the descendants of cooperating prokaryotic cells. Eukaryotic organelles like mitochondria and chloroplasts contain their own DNA separate from the nucleus, suggesting they were indeed once separate cells that came along for the ride.

23

16 PUT AWAY THAT DNA!

If you've ever had trouble stuffing toys into a box, socks into a drawer or fourteen swimsuits into a beach vacation suitcase, you could learn a lot from your chromosomes.

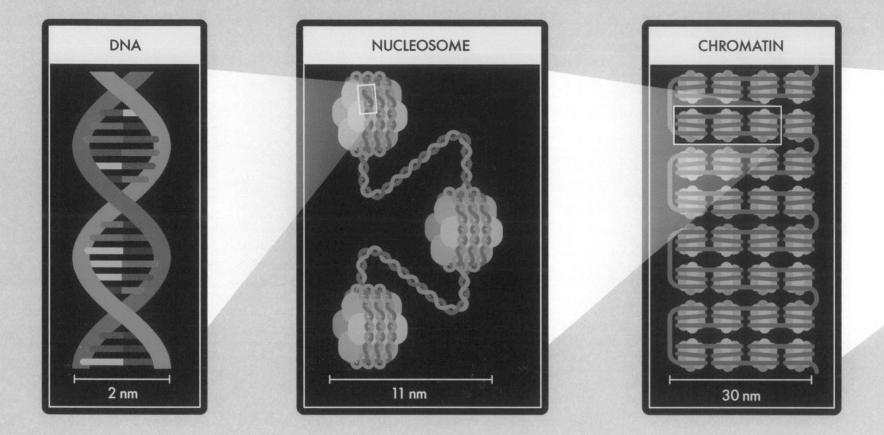

DNA	NUCLEOSOME	CHROMATIN
2 nm	11 nm	30 nm

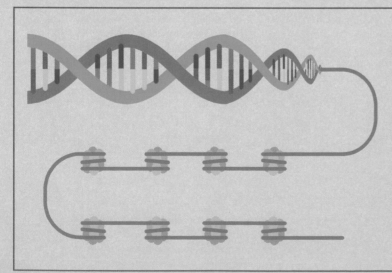

Luckily, your cells have a packing system, and it's very good. First, the DNA gets wrapped around proteins called histones. Eight histone proteins clamp together and hold DNA coiled tight around them, in a structure called a *nucleosome* (NEW-klee-oh-zome). With free DNA between them, these nucleosomes look like "beads on a string" under a microscope.

But your DNA doesn't just sit there, looking like a necklace you made in summer camp. That's just the first step. Next, the Oreo-shaped nucleosomes stack up and coil into a tightly-packed mass called a chromatin fiber. Though this fiber is only about 15 times wider than "free" double-stranded DNA, it packs an incredible amount of material into a small space.

DOI: 10.4324/9781003292111-16

The chromosomes in each of your cells have a physics problem. They live in a nucleus, which has a diameter of around 5–10 picometers, where a picometer is one-trillionth of a meter. The DNA that has to fit there, if stretched out fully, would be roughly two meters long. You couldn't cram all that in there with a million shoehorns.

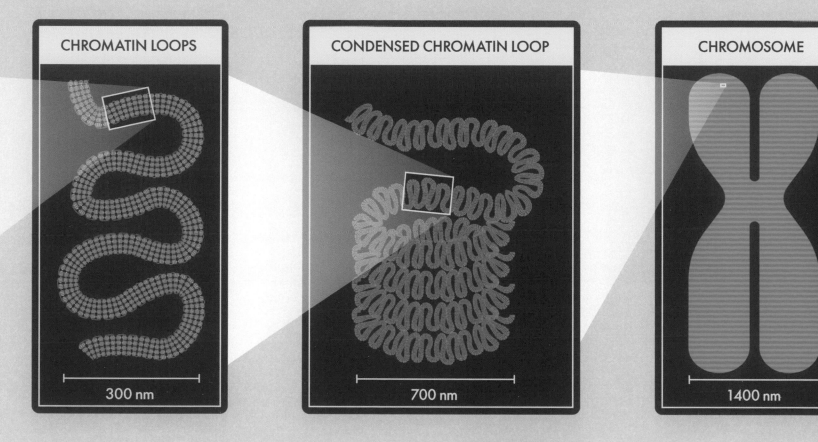

CHROMATIN LOOPS

300 nm

CONDENSED CHROMATIN LOOP

700 nm

CHROMOSOME

1400 nm

DON'T SHUT THAT SUITCASE YET!

Your DNA condenses much further still. The chromatin fibers act like a computer cable or extension cord, and bend and coil in on themselves to reduce even more space. Finally, this tangled mess—the coil of coiled coils—folds even further and forms a chromosome, condensed thousands of times smaller than the original DNA.

25

FAMILY REUNIONS ARE BANANAS (LITERALLY)

Ah, the humble banana. Sometimes it's a quick breakfast while you're running for your bus. Other times, it's a smashed mess that you "discover" at the bottom of your backpack. But the truth is, we should give a banana more respect than we do because it—and everything that grows, creeps, and crawls on Earth (or inside your backpack, for that matter)—is part of our family tree, in the genetic sense.

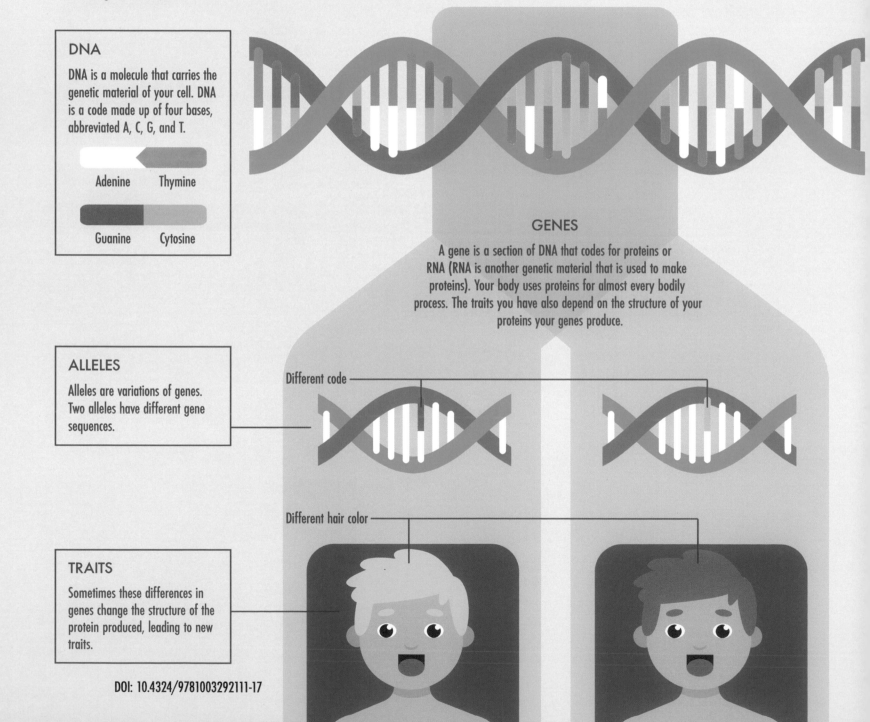

DNA

DNA is a molecule that carries the genetic material of your cell. DNA is a code made up of four bases, abbreviated A, C, G, and T.

Adenine   Thymine

Guanine   Cytosine

GENES

A gene is a section of DNA that codes for proteins or RNA (RNA is another genetic material that is used to make proteins). Your body uses proteins for almost every bodily process. The traits you have also depend on the structure of your proteins your genes produce.

ALLELES

Alleles are variations of genes. Two alleles have different gene sequences.

Different code

Different hair color

TRAITS

Sometimes these differences in genes change the structure of the protein produced, leading to new traits.

DOI: 10.4324/9781003292111-17

Our DNA holds the key to the largest family tree on Earth. New species evolve from existing species. That means that humans are related to every species on Earth (even that smashed banana in your backpack).

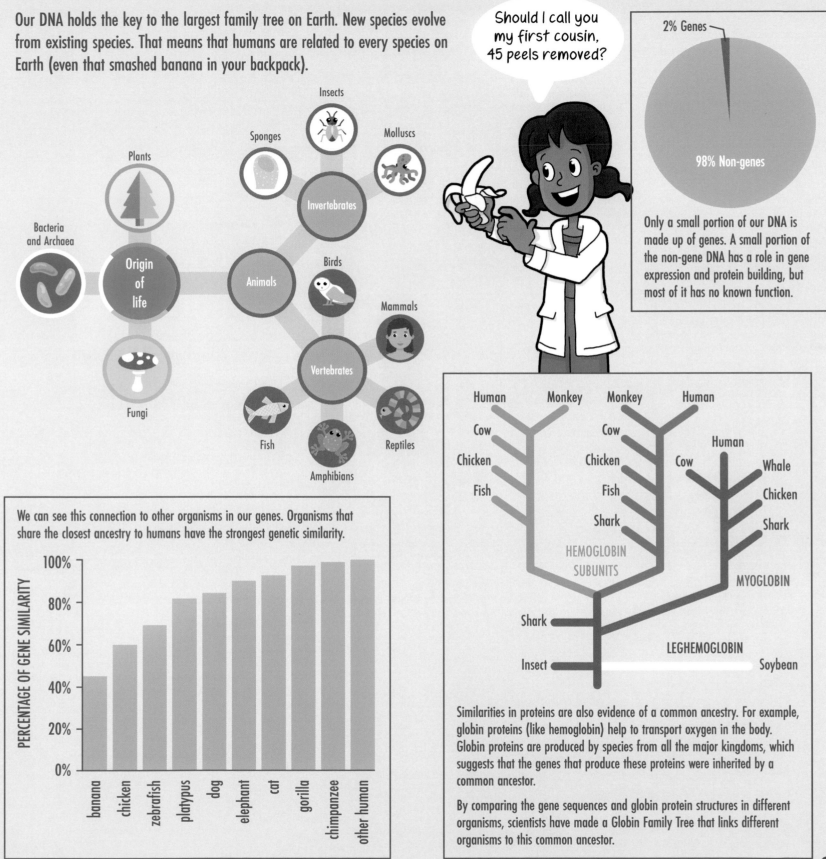

Should I call you my first cousin, 45 peels removed?

2% Genes

98% Non-genes

Only a small portion of our DNA is made up of genes. A small portion of the non-gene DNA has a role in gene expression and protein building, but most of it has no known function.

Plants

Sponges

Insects

Molluscs

Bacteria and Archaea

Origin of life

Invertebrates

Animals

Birds

Mammals

Fungi

Vertebrates

Fish

Amphibians

Reptiles

We can see this connection to other organisms in our genes. Organisms that share the closest ancestry to humans have the strongest genetic similarity.

PERCENTAGE OF GENE SIMILARITY

100%
80%
60%
40%
20%
0%

banana
chicken
zebrafish
platypus
dog
elephant
cat
gorilla
chimpanzee
other human

Human   Monkey   Monkey   Human

Cow   Cow

Chicken   Chicken   Human

Fish   Fish   Cow   Whale

                        Shark   Chicken

Shark   Shark

HEMOGLOBIN SUBUNITS

                                         MYOGLOBIN

Shark

                         LEGHEMOGLOBIN

Insect   Soybean

Similarities in proteins are also evidence of a common ancestry. For example, globin proteins (like hemoglobin) help to transport oxygen in the body. Globin proteins are produced by species from all the major kingdoms, which suggests that the genes that produce these proteins were inherited by a common ancestor.

By comparing the gene sequences and globin protein structures in different organisms, scientists have made a Globin Family Tree that links different organisms to this common ancestor.

18 TOO MUCH OF A GOOD GENE?

Our DNA includes around 30,000 genes, which together produce all the proteins to build our cells, tissues, organs, and bodies. So, genes are pretty important. But the protein-producing bits of genes only make up about 1–2% of our total DNA. So, what's the rest of it?

Some of our "extra" DNA looks very different than genes. Telomeres, for example, are regions that protect the ends of chromosomes, and regulatory elements of various kinds help control how and when certain genes are put to work. But a lot of the in-between-gene DNA *looks* like genes—but isn't, quite. These are the remnants and ghosts of gene copies.

New copies of existing genes get added to the genome in several ways. For instance, when DNA from parents is recombined during meiosis, misalignment of the chromosomes from mother and father can lead to two separate copies of the same gene being passed down. These copies—and copies of other genes—can accumulate over many generations.

If the original version of the gene functions properly, the copies may have no use in cells. Depending on where in the genome they land, the copies may be unable to produce proteins at all. Over time, these "extra" genes may pick up mutations and fall into disrepair, effectively shut off by the cells. These non-functional copies are called pseudogenes, and our genomes now contain approximately as many of these "false" genes as protein-coding genes.

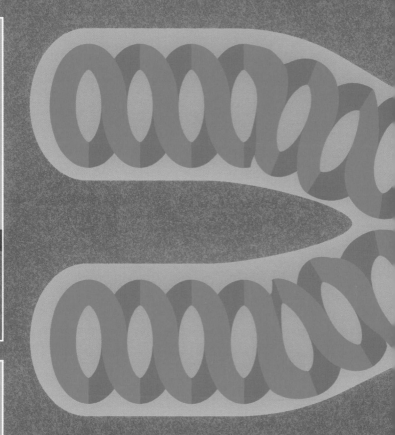

DOI: 10.4324/9781003292111-18

Another way gene copies can emerge involves RNA. To produce a protein, a gene must first be read, or transcribed, into RNA. During this process, stretches of non-coding DNA called introns are snipped out of the RNA sequence, leaving a shorter, streamlined sequence ready to be translated into a protein. This is the process that produces all of the proteins in our cells.

Under certain conditions, though, RNA can be "retrotransposed" into the genome. The "retro" bit means the RNA is converted "back" to DNA—but without the introns, so it doesn't look exactly like the original gene, either. This "processed" copy of the gene is then "transposed", or integrated into a different random spot, somewhere on the genome. Over time, retrotransposed genes may lose function (if they ever had any) and also become pseudogenes.

Retrotransposition (and transposition, which involves only DNA) happens quite a lot in our genomes, and those of many other species. Transposable elements (or transposons, or TEs for short) sit within our genomes and ping-pong themselves into different locations from time to time, sometimes dragging innocent RNA (or DNA) sequence along with them. These "jumping genes" have transposed so much, in fact, that around 45% of our DNA is now made of TEs.

Uh, so are you going to introduce me to your friends?

19 HOX ROCKS!

Have you ever wondered how your body knew where your head should be placed? Or why your pet doesn't have its tail growing out of its head? The answer is in little segments of DNA called Hox genes.

Hox genes provide the blueprint for an organism's body. They tell the body how to build certain body parts and provide instructions on where these structures should be placed.

FLY

MOUSE

HUMAN

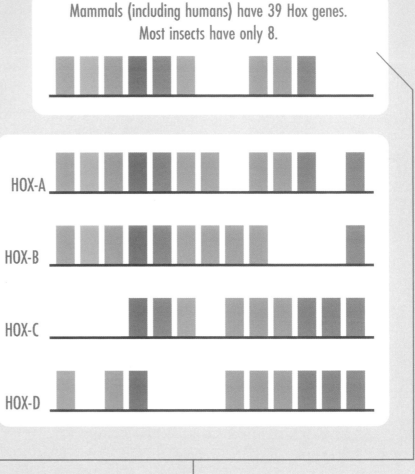

Mammals (including humans) have 39 Hox genes. Most insects have only 8.

HOX-A

HOX-B

HOX-C

HOX-D

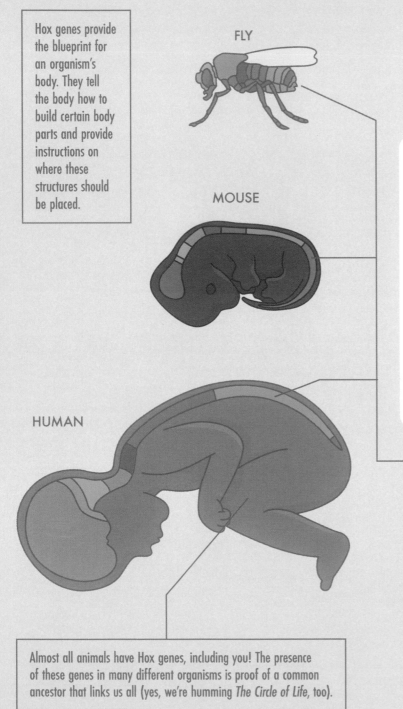

Even though the number of Hox genes differ, there are certain types of Hox genes that control the development of a certain body part in all organisms. That means that the types of Hox genes that make an insect rear-end are the same types that make a mouse rear-end. (It's an odd specialty to have, but the Hox genes are sticking to it.)

Almost all animals have Hox genes, including you! The presence of these genes in many different organisms is proof of a common ancestor that links us all (yes, we're humming *The Circle of Life*, too).

DOI: 10.4324/9781003292111-19

BALANCED ON THE HEDGE

If you're a fan of iconic video games, you probably remember certain characters well. But whether you battled with Bowser, sighted a Snorlax or legged out legends with Link, we can guarantee you grew up with sonic hedgehog.

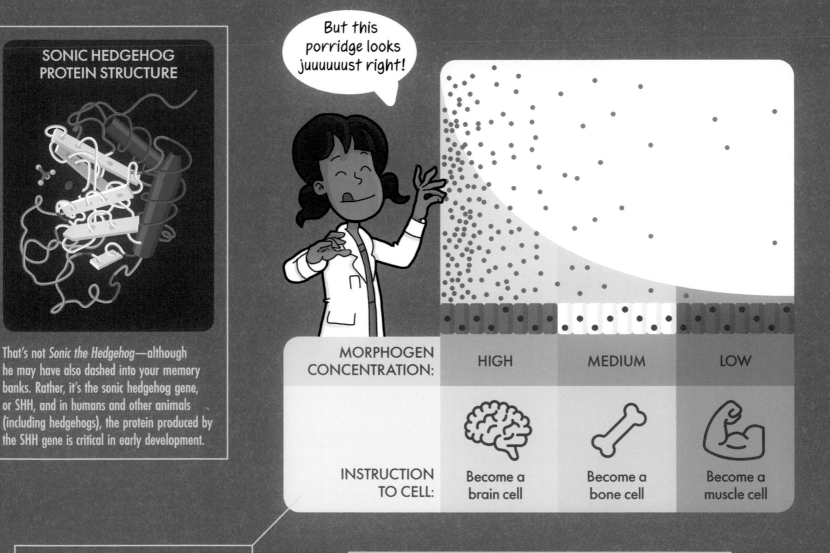

SONIC HEDGEHOG PROTEIN STRUCTURE

That's not *Sonic the Hedgehog*—although he may have also dashed into your memory banks. Rather, it's the sonic hedgehog gene, or SHH, and in humans and other animals (including hedgehogs), the protein produced by the SHH gene is critical in early development.

But this porridge looks juuuuuust right!

MORPHOGEN CONCENTRATION:	HIGH	MEDIUM	LOW
INSTRUCTION TO CELL:	Become a brain cell	Become a bone cell	Become a muscle cell

The sonic hedgehog protein is a morphogen (MORF-o-gin), meaning it has different effects depending on how much is present in a given cell. As in the picture at right, high levels of protein can cause cells to develop in one way, while lower levels in other cells may lead them down a different path of development.

In many animals, levels of sonic hedgehog and other proteins regulate how cells develop and grow in embryos' brains, eyes and limbs, among other tissues. If too much or too little SHH is expressed, or expressed at the wrong time, these tissues could fail to develop, overdevelop (producing extra fingers, for example) or, in adults, lead to conditions including cancer.

DOI: 10.4324/9781003292111-20

TELO ME YOUR LIFE STORY

21

All good things must come to an end. That's true for chromosomes, for cells and for people—and it turns out, the end of each one may be closely related.

In each of your trillions of cells, the DNA is packed into 23 pairs of chromosomes. When those cells divide—as most of them do during your lifetime to keep you growing and healthy, about 50 times each on average—all the chromosomes are copied, so each new cell has a full set of DNA.

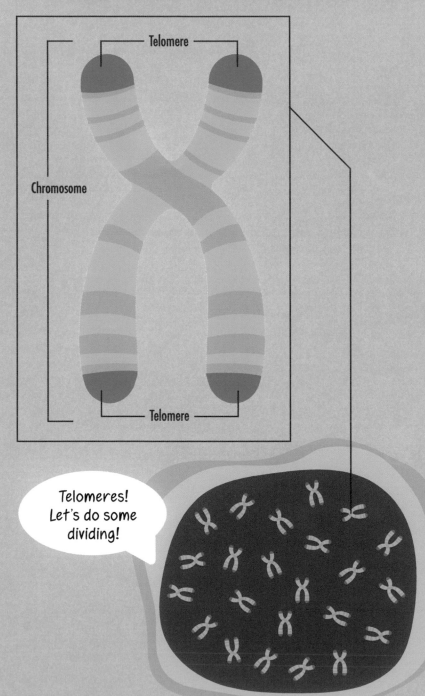

Chromosome

Telomere

Telomere

Telomeres! Let's do some dividing!

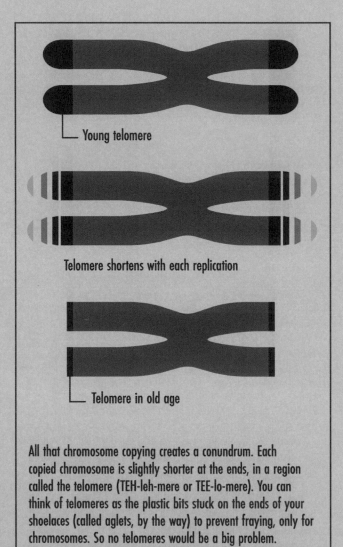

Young telomere

Telomere shortens with each replication

Telomere in old age

All that chromosome copying creates a conundrum. Each copied chromosome is slightly shorter at the ends, in a region called the telomere (TEH-leh-mere or TEE-lo-mere). You can think of telomeres as the plastic bits stuck on the ends of your shoelaces (called aglets, by the way) to prevent fraying, only for chromosomes. So no telomeres would be a big problem.

When the telomeres of a cell's chromosomes get too short, that cell can no longer divide. It will gradually suffer DNA and cellular damage that can't be repaired, and the cell will die. As the telomeres go, so goes the cell—and any chance of dividing into more cells.

DOI: 10.4324/9781003292111-21

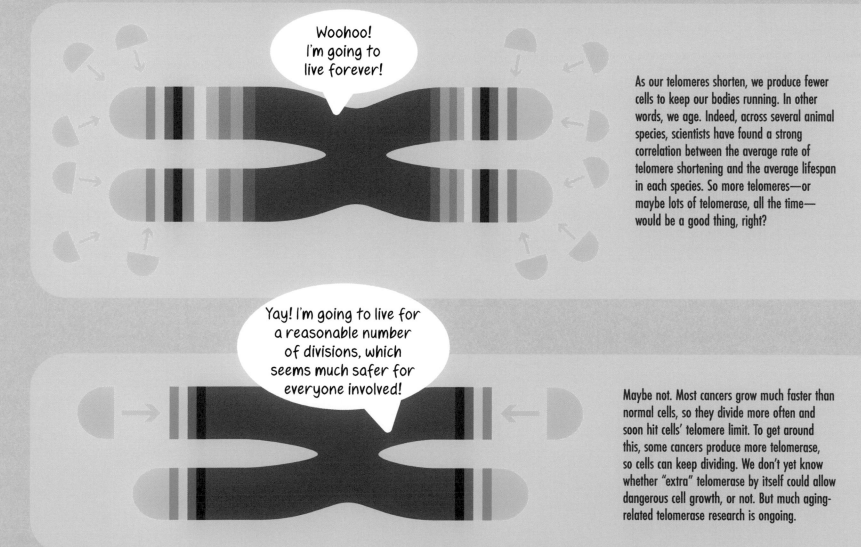

Shaving down telomeres isn't a one-way process, luckily. In sperm and egg cells, an enzyme called *telomerase* (tell-AHM-er-ace) rebuilds telomeres, so these cells can divide over and over again. Telomerase also acts in most of our other cells, but at much lower levels, so our bodies gradually lose the ability to grow and heal and repair with new cells over time.

As our telomeres shorten, we produce fewer cells to keep our bodies running. In other words, we age. Indeed, across several animal species, scientists have found a strong correlation between the average rate of telomere shortening and the average lifespan in each species. So more telomeres—or maybe lots of telomerase, all the time— would be a good thing, right?

Maybe not. Most cancers grow much faster than normal cells, so they divide more often and soon hit cells' telomere limit. To get around this, some cancers produce more telomerase, so cells can keep dividing. We don't yet know whether "extra" telomerase by itself could allow dangerous cell growth, or not. But much aging-related telomerase research is ongoing.

JUST HERE TO INTERFERE

Every cell in your body contains around 30,000 genes. In each of those cells, a subset of genes is "expressed", their message converted from DNA to RNA and finally to the proteins that form the cell's structures and carry out important functions. Which genes are expressed—and when—determines whether the cell is a neuron or a red blood cell or a bit of pinky toe skin.

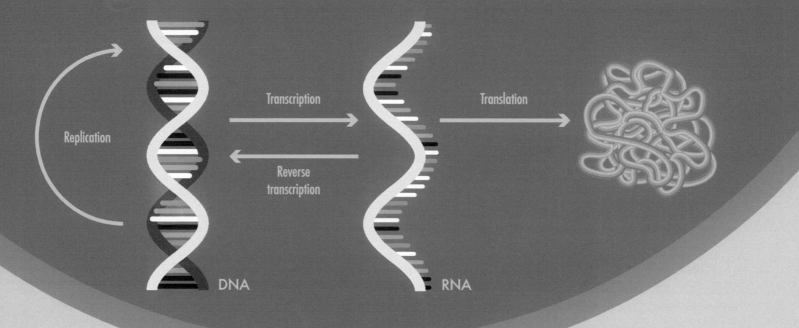

Replication

Transcription

Reverse transcription

Translation

DNA

RNA

The "when" can be very important. Some proteins are needed only early in a cell's development, for instance. Think about building a house—once the main structure is finished, there's little use for more bricks. They won't help much when it's time to put in the kitchen sink. So how does a cell turn off, or down, expression of a gene? One way is with RNA interference.

STOP

STOP

Translation

Nix the bricks! Nix the bricks quick!

DOI: 10.4324/9781003292111-22

RNA interference, or RNAi for short, is performed by short strands of RNA produced by "non-coding" genes, so called because their RNAs don't produce proteins—they exist only to get in the way of other RNAs. If the sequence of a non-coding RNA matches a portion of a coding RNA sequence, the interfering RNA will latch on—and that's bad news for gene expression.

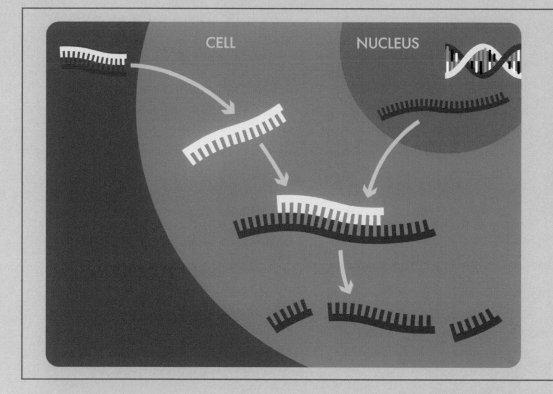

Our interfering RNAs can regulate gene expression in several ways, and the targets may be human RNAs or RNAs of certain invading viruses. One strategy gets right to the point: some non-coding RNAs bring along a protein that chops coding RNAs into small bits, which can't produce proteins. It's the old "walk softly and carry a big paper shredder" approach.

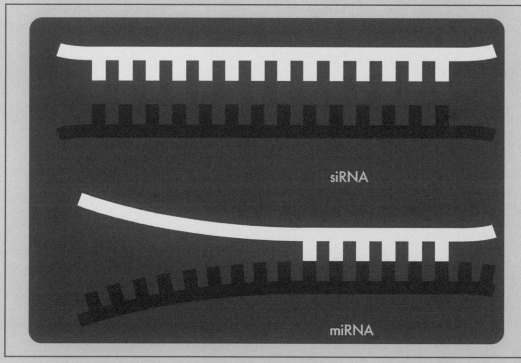

Each of your cells contains hundreds of interfering RNA genes, which come in two "flavors": small interfering RNAs (or siRNAs) regulate a specific coding gene or RNA, while microRNAs (or miRNAs) are less specific, and may bind and regulate many genes. Researchers also engineer RNAi for use in research, by designing new sequences based on genes of interest.

WHEN YOUR HONKER IS HONKING

Have you ever noticed that one side of your nose gets stuffier than the other? It isn't your imagination. It has to do with a normal cycle that happens inside your nose.

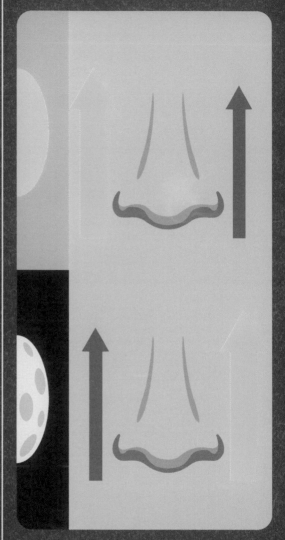

Your nostrils work as a tag team. One side takes more air than the other. About 4 to 8 hours later, the nostrils switch off, and the other nostril takes in more air.

This nostril tag-team may strengthen your sense of smell. Scientists found that the high-airflow nostril and the low-airflow nostril send different smell signals to the brain. The brain processes these two different signals and determines how to react.

When you have a cold, your nose produces extra snot and mucus. The high-airflow nostril can clear most of this gunk, but the low-airflow nostril gets congested and stuffy, at least until the nostrils switch sides.

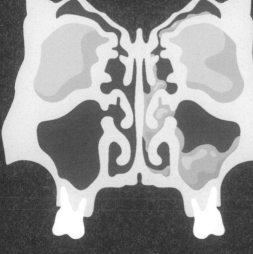

Cover your nose!

DOI: 10.4324/9781003292111-23

UGH, BRAIN FREEZE!

Have you ever slurped down a cold, refreshing glass of ice water only to be hit with an aching head? Whether you call it brain freeze or ice-cream headache, this mysterious reaction is enough to make scientists' heads hurt.

The scientific name for brain freeze is *sphenopalatine ganglioneuralgia* (pronunciation: sfen-nuh-PA-la-teen gang-glee-oh-nur-Al-gee-ah. Whew!). Which, admittedly, sounds like a Star Wars villain. But this long name refers to the group of nerve cells that likely cause brain freeze.

Scientists think that brain freeze happens when something very cold hits the roof of your mouth. This sensation triggers cold receptors in this region.

The cold temperatures cause blood vessels in this area to constrict.

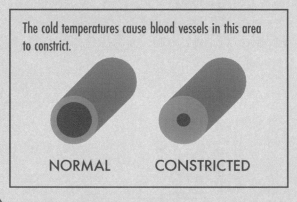

NORMAL   CONSTRICTED

This constriction triggers the trigeminal nerve, which sends a pain signal to the brain. You feel this pain in your forehead or temple region. The pain goes away in seconds or minutes. It can also be relieved by taking in warm air or by eating something warm.

■ Affected by brain freeze

■ Not affected by brain freeze

35%

65%

Brain freeze is puzzling to scientists because not everyone gets it. Research shows that people who get migraines—a severe type of headache—seem to be more likely to get brain freeze than people who do not.

DOI: 10.4324/9781003292111-24

25 NERVES MADE FOR SPEED

Touch this page. Did you feel the texture of the paper immediately? This happens because the nerves in your finger send signals to and from your brain at incredibly fast speeds—so fast, that you don't even notice it.

DENDRITES
Pick up signal from another neuron

AXON TERMINAL BUNDLE
Sends message to neuron

AXON
Electrical signal travels

Neurons are cells that make up your nerves. These cells carry messages to and from your brain.

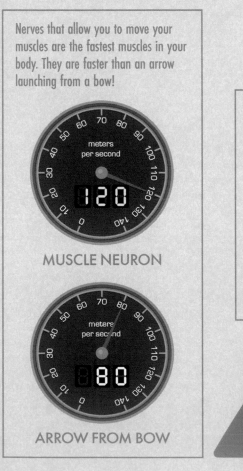

Nerves that allow you to move your muscles are the fastest muscles in your body. They are faster than an arrow launching from a bow!

meters per second

120

MUSCLE NEURON

meters per second

80

ARROW FROM BOW

The neurons that sense heat or pain are much slower, with a maximum speed of about 2 meters per second (about 4 miles per hour). Have you ever scraped your knee while playing, but you didn't feel the pain until a few moments later? These slower neurons are the reason.

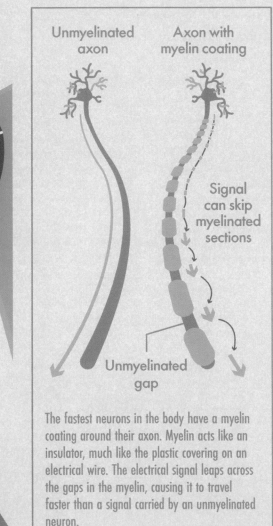

Unmyelinated axon

Axon with myelin coating

Signal can skip myelinated sections

Unmyelinated gap

The fastest neurons in the body have a myelin coating around their axon. Myelin acts like an insulator, much like the plastic covering on an electrical wire. The electrical signal leaps across the gaps in the myelin, causing it to travel faster than a signal carried by an unmyelinated neuron.

DOI: 10.4324/9781003292111-25

HUMAN SEE, HUMAN DO

Your friend yawns. Seconds later, you yawn, too. Coincidence? Nope! Yawning—and a bunch of other human behaviors—are contagious due to the mirror neuron system in the brain.

Mirror neurons are so named because they cause a person to mimic the actions of the person they are watching. This helps us to build social bonds and relate to others. Mirror neurons are activated when you observe others yawn, laugh, itch, and express different emotions.

Mirror neurons are found in other animals, like birds. A sparrow will sing if it hears the song of another sparrow.

1 When you see your friend yawn, your eyes send this information to the brain.

2 The part of the brain that processes the yawn sends a signal to the mirror neuron system in your brain.

3 The mirror neuron system processes the yawn and responds with "Well, we must yawn, too!" So it sends the signal that makes you feel a yawn coming on. Your yawn shows empathy, specifically that you relate to your friends' needs (the need for a nap).

2:
You must be tired.

Human input to mirror neuron system

Visual input to mirror neuron system

I:
I see you yawn.

3:
I can relate to that.
Watch this...

DOI: 10.4324/9781003292111-26

39

27 THE THINKER IS A SHRINKER

Ever made a "big brain" move in a video game? Well, you better enjoy the bigness of your brain, now. As you age, your brain shrinks. As it turns out, this shrinkage makes humans quite odd compared to our closest animal relatives.

Babies are the real "big brains" among us, at least compared to the size of the rest of their body. The brain is only about 2% of an adult's body's weight, compared to about 10% of an infant's body weight.

Newborn   Child   Adult

The volume inside your cranium consists of your brain and brain fluids. After age 40, this volume shrinks. Scientists believe this is due to the death of neurons and other age-related changes in the brain.

CRANIUM CAPACITY

AGE

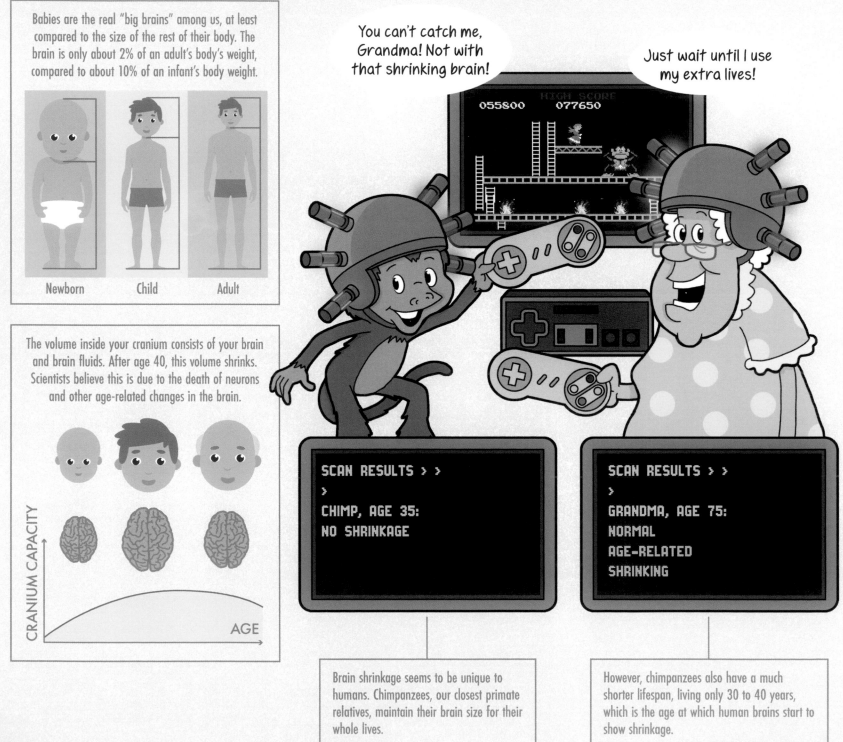

You can't catch me, Grandma! Not with that shrinking brain!

Just wait until I use my extra lives!

HIGH SCORE
055800   077650

SCAN RESULTS > >
>
CHIMP, AGE 35:
NO SHRINKAGE

SCAN RESULTS > >
>
GRANDMA, AGE 75:
NORMAL
AGE-RELATED
SHRINKING

Brain shrinkage seems to be unique to humans. Chimpanzees, our closest primate relatives, maintain their brain size for their whole lives.

However, chimpanzees also have a much shorter lifespan, living only 30 to 40 years, which is the age at which human brains start to show shrinkage.

40

DOI: 10.4324/9781003292111-27

Oddly, our brains do not shrink uniformly. Most of the shrinkage occurs in two sections: the hippocampus and the frontal lobe. These changes can lead to mild changes in memory and brain function as we age.

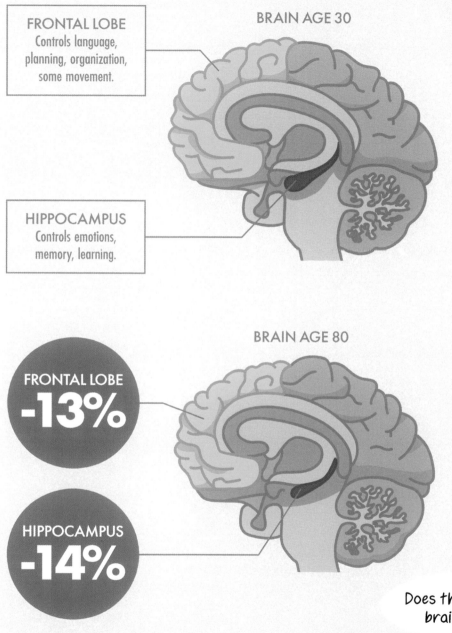

FRONTAL LOBE
Controls language, planning, organization, some movement.

BRAIN AGE 30

HIPPOCAMPUS
Controls emotions, memory, learning.

BRAIN AGE 80

FRONTAL LOBE
-13%

HIPPOCAMPUS
-14%

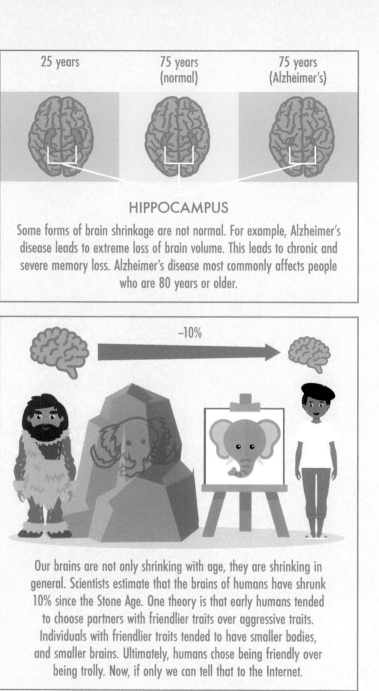

| 25 years | 75 years (normal) | 75 years (Alzheimer's) |

HIPPOCAMPUS

Some forms of brain shrinkage are not normal. For example, Alzheimer's disease leads to extreme loss of brain volume. This leads to chronic and severe memory loss. Alzheimer's disease most commonly affects people who are 80 years or older.

−10%

Our brains are not only shrinking with age, they are shrinking in general. Scientists estimate that the brains of humans have shrunk 10% since the Stone Age. One theory is that early humans tended to choose partners with friendlier traits over aggressive traits. Individuals with friendlier traits tended to have smaller bodies, and smaller brains. Ultimately, humans chose being friendly over being trolly. Now, if only we can tell that to the Internet.

NORMAL EFFECTS OF AGING
* Mild forgetfulness (forgetting keys, or the name of a person they just met).
* Multitasking becomes more difficult.
* Takes longer to process new information.

However, a person's skills and knowledge are unaffected by age and may actually improve over time.

Does this hat make my brain look small?

28 YOU STEM FROM STEM CELLS

As you grow, your body needs to make more cells, so that there can be more of, well, *you*. Even when you stop growing taller, your body will make new cells to replace dead cells. To do this, your body uses microscopic cell factories called stem cells.

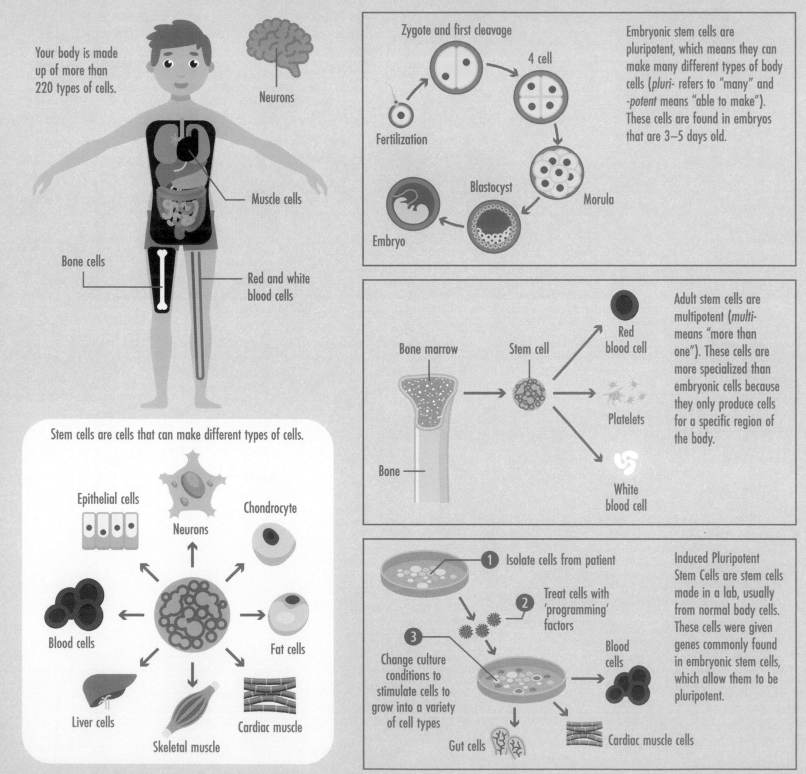

Your body is made up of more than 220 types of cells.

Neurons

Muscle cells

Bone cells

Red and white blood cells

Stem cells are cells that can make different types of cells.

Epithelial cells
Neurons
Chondrocyte
Blood cells
Fat cells
Liver cells
Skeletal muscle
Cardiac muscle

Zygote and first cleavage

Fertilization

4 cell

Morula

Blastocyst

Embryo

Embryonic stem cells are pluripotent, which means they can make many different types of body cells (*pluri-* refers to "many" and *-potent* means "able to make"). These cells are found in embryos that are 3–5 days old.

Bone marrow

Stem cell

Red blood cell

Platelets

White blood cell

Bone

Adult stem cells are multipotent (*multi-* means "more than one"). These cells are more specialized than embryonic cells because they only produce cells for a specific region of the body.

1 Isolate cells from patient

2 Treat cells with 'programming' factors

3 Change culture conditions to stimulate cells to grow into a variety of cell types

Blood cells

Gut cells

Cardiac muscle cells

Induced Pluripotent Stem Cells are stem cells made in a lab, usually from normal body cells. These cells were given genes commonly found in embryonic stem cells, which allow them to be pluripotent.

DOI: 10.4324/9781003292111-28

USING STEM CELLS TO TREAT HEALTH PROBLEMS

Stem cells are currently used to treat certain injuries and disease, and more exciting treatments are on the horizon.

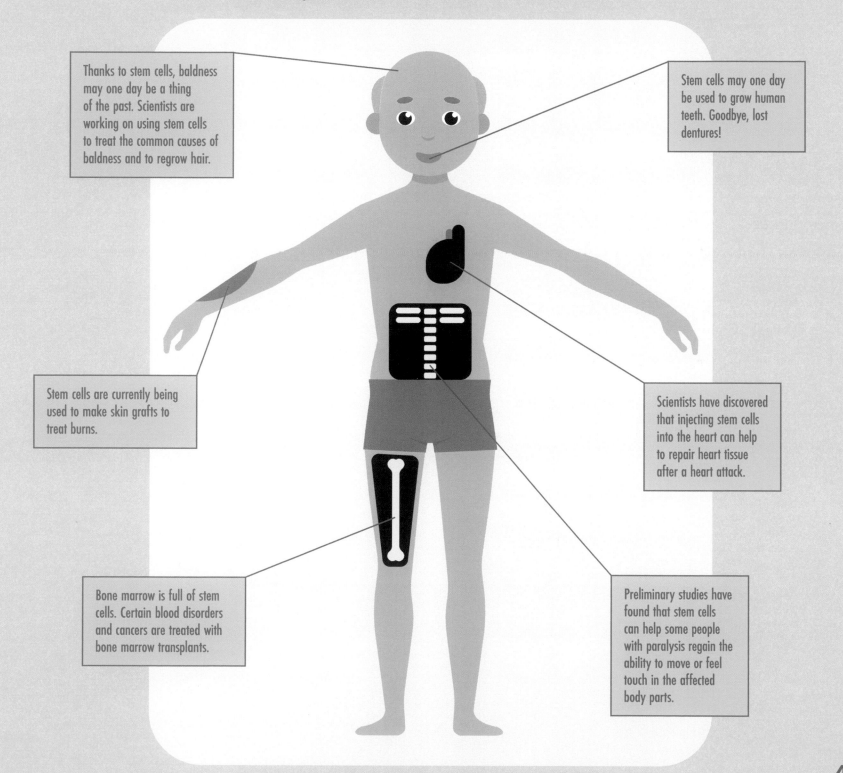

Thanks to stem cells, baldness may one day be a thing of the past. Scientists are working on using stem cells to treat the common causes of baldness and to regrow hair.

Stem cells may one day be used to grow human teeth. Goodbye, lost dentures!

Stem cells are currently being used to make skin grafts to treat burns.

Scientists have discovered that injecting stem cells into the heart can help to repair heart tissue after a heart attack.

Bone marrow is full of stem cells. Certain blood disorders and cancers are treated with bone marrow transplants.

Preliminary studies have found that stem cells can help some people with paralysis regain the ability to move or feel touch in the affected body parts.

 **29**

REDUCE, REUSE, RECYCLE

The kidneys are your body's recycling plants. They remove toxins, conserve vitamins, and help with water balance. But how much do you really know about this weird pair of organs?

Your kidneys' main function is to filter waste from the bloodstream and produce urine from this waste. Your kidneys filter about 37.5 gallons of blood per day. That's a lot of work for these small organs!

6.4"

5"

37.5 gallons

NEPHRON WORKS

1 Blood enters the kidney for waste removal.

2 Nephrons are the parts of the kidney that filter waste and produce urine. First, the nephron takes in water, glucose, salt, and other small molecules from the capillaries.

4 The blood is filtered one more time. This time, waste from medication, extra hydrogen and potassium ions, and other substances enter the kidney.

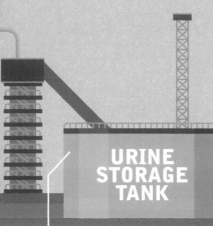

URINE STORAGE TANK

3 Some water, nutrients, and sugars are delivered back to the blood for use by the body.

5 The kidney produces urine from this waste. This urine is shuttled to the bladder for removal during your next bathroom trip.

44

DOI: 10.4324/9781003292111-29

You only need one kidney to survive. In fact, people with unilateral renal agenesis are only born with one kidney. Usually, their kidney grows to the size of two kidneys.

Some people donate one of their kidneys to a person who has health issues with their kidneys.

DONOR

Donor kidney

Incision

Bladder

RECIPIENT

Diseased kidneys

Transplanted kidney

Bladder

"One-sided"   "an organ that doesn't form"

UNILATERAL RENAL AGENESIS

"Kidney"

3% Uric acid

2% Urea

95% Water

PARTICULARLY PEE-CULIAR . . .

HOLD YOUR NOSE IF YOU EAT ASPARAGUS
Asparagus contains a chemical called asparagusic acid, which breaks down into smelly sulfur chemicals. This causes your pee to have an especially stinky smell.

THERE ARE BAGS OF PEE ON THE MOON
There are no port-a-potties for the astronauts who visited the Moon, so some bags of pee (and poop) were left behind.

BUILDING A PEE PENTHOUSE
Engineering students from University of Cape Town (UCT) in South Africa designed bricks made from human urine. The bricks are safe to handle and have no "pee smell". One brick required about 25 liters of urine, which equals about 100–125 trips to the bathroom.

Your urine is mostly water. Urea is a waste product that forms when your body breaks down proteins. Urea can also form ammonia, which gives pee its characteristic smell.

45

A NIFTY TRIP FROM CRYPT TO TIP

We may not give them much thought, but our intestines are constantly working for us, absorbing nutrients from the food we eat to keep our bodies running. In our small intestines, this nutrient nabbing is performed by villi, tiny finger-like blobs of cells that dangle inside the intestine, scooping up the tasty vitamins and fluids floating by.

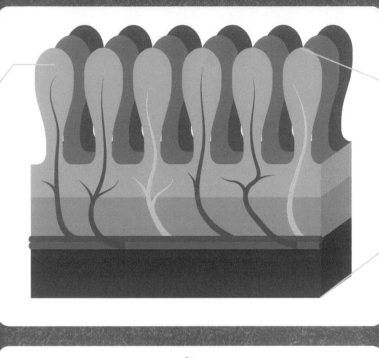

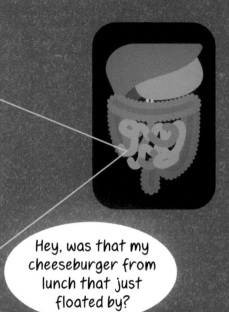

These villi are tiny—about as long as a penny is thick. In order to trap more particles, the outer cells in each villus grow even tinier hair-like ridges called microvilli, which increase the grub-grabbing surface by 600 fold. Every day, our villi collect vital nutrients and absorb two gallons of fluids, mostly with their "hair". Even Marge Simpson couldn't manage that.

Hey, was that my cheeseburger from lunch that just floated by?

VILLUS TIP

CRYPT

At the base of the villi are "crypts", where hundreds of millions of new intestinal cells are produced in each of our bodies every day. Cells near the crypts produce antibiotics to protect against infection, while cells further up absorb sugars and cells further up still absorb fats. Cells at the tips also help to regulate the body's immune response to the bacteria living in our guts.

Amazingly, recent research shows that all these different kinds of cells are... the same cells! As the young cells at the bottom of villi mature and migrate toward the tip, they constantly change their function based on their location. It takes just four days for cells to emerge, go through their whirlwind of changes, reach the tip and fall off, to be absorbed by villi downstream. Life can be pretty gruesome when you're born in a crypt, we guess.

DOI: 10.4324/9781003292111-30

HUMAN PRINT QUEUE

Bioprinting is the use of 3D printing to build artificial tissues and organs. In the not-so-distant future, this technology may be used to create organs for organ transplants and repair or replace diseased cells or organs. Let's take a look at how it works.

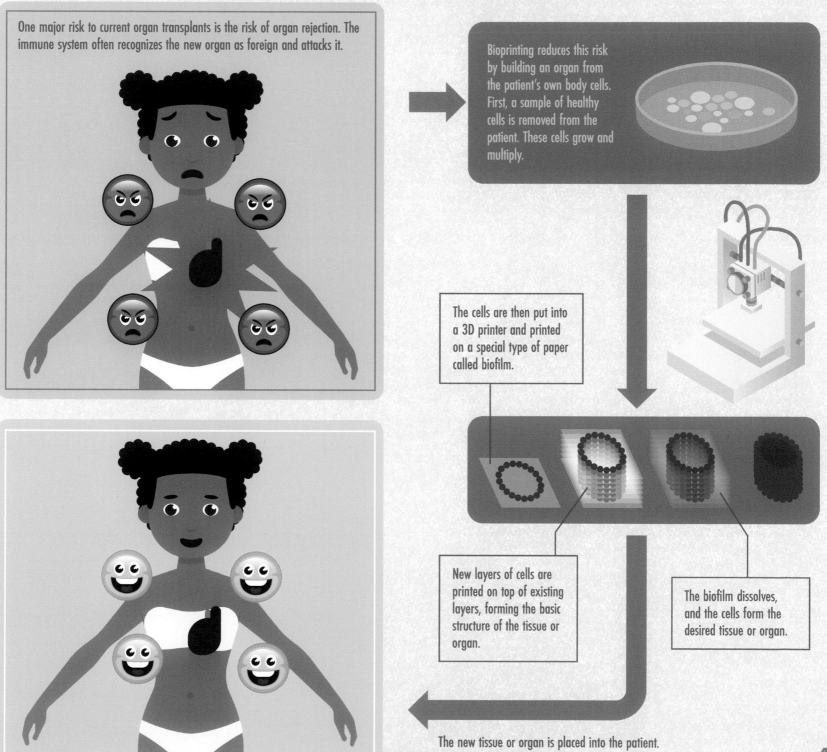

One major risk to current organ transplants is the risk of organ rejection. The immune system often recognizes the new organ as foreign and attacks it.

Bioprinting reduces this risk by building an organ from the patient's own body cells. First, a sample of healthy cells is removed from the patient. These cells grow and multiply.

The cells are then put into a 3D printer and printed on a special type of paper called biofilm.

New layers of cells are printed on top of existing layers, forming the basic structure of the tissue or organ.

The biofilm dissolves, and the cells form the desired tissue or organ.

The new tissue or organ is placed into the patient.

DOI: 10.4324/9781003292111-31

32 ENDO? EXO? WHO CRINE FIGURE THIS OUT?

The job of glands is to spew substances your body needs (or more than you need, if you have a lot of snot due to a cold. The glands can be a little *too* generous, sometimes.) But what exactly oozes out of these glands? And why do we need this ooze? Let's take a closer look at these oozy parts of our bodies.

DOI: 10.4324/9781003292111-32

There are two main types of glands:

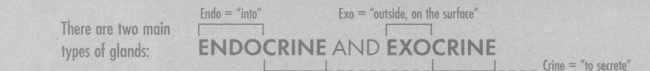

Endo = "into"   Exo = "outside, on the surface"

ENDOCRINE AND **EXOCRINE**

Crine = "to secrete"

ENDOCRINE Endocrine glands secrete hormones and other substances into the blood. These glands do not have ducts.

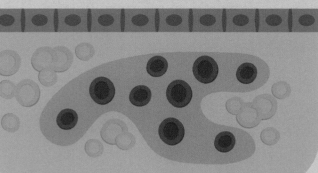

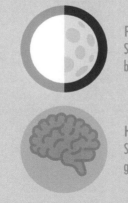

THYROID GLAND
SECRETES: Two hormones that play vital roles in metabolism, heart function and muscle control.

PINEAL GLAND
SECRETES: Melatonin, a hormone that helps your body sleep.

HYPOTHALAMUS
SECRETES: Many different hormones that affect mood, growth, water balance and sleep cycles.

EXOCRINE Exocrine glands secrete substances through ducts to epithelial tissue. Epithelial tissue lines body surfaces and organs.

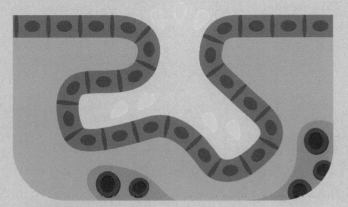

SWEAT GLAND
PRODUCE: Sweat.
FUNCTION: Cools the body when the water evaporates.

SALIVARY GLANDS
PRODUCE: Saliva.
FUNCTION: Softens and digests food.

MUCOUS GLANDS
PRODUCE: Mucous.
FUNCTION: Coats and protects body surfaces.

Some organs, like the pancreas and liver, work double-duty—
they are both endocrine and exocrine glands.

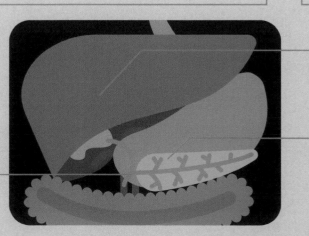

Exocrine duct tissue

LIVER
EXOCRINE: Secretes bile, which helps digest fats.
ENDOCRINE: Secretes hormones that control blood pressure and stimulate growth of the body.

PANCREAS
ENDOCRINE: Secretes insulin, a hormone that controls blood sugar levels.
EXOCRINE: Secretes enzymes into the small intestine that help digest food.

33 KEEP THE BEAT

In the past year, your heart has beaten 35 million times. (Maybe a little more, if you're a fan of roller coasters or scary movies.) Most of the cells in your heart are the strong, silent type, good at taking orders. When the signal comes to pump, they pump. But where does that signal come from, and how does it stay so steady (at least until the coaster reaches the top of a hill)?

Some cells, like those in muscles and nerves, can pass an electrical signal from one end to the other, and on to a neighboring cell. They do so by allowing chemical elements called ions with tiny electrical charges into or out of the cell to keep the signal flowing. But only a few cells have "automaticity" (ah-toe-mah-TISS-ih-tee), meaning they can generate a signal on their own.

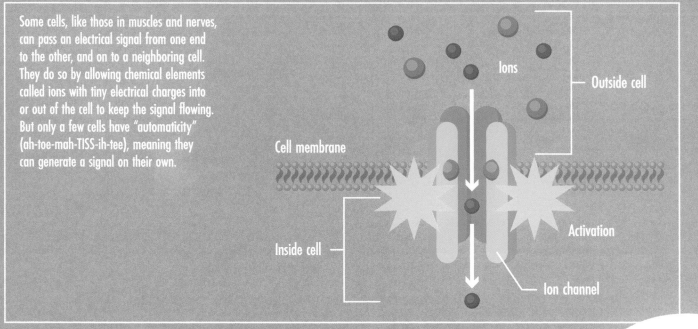

Ions

Outside cell

Cell membrane

Inside cell

Activation

Ion channel

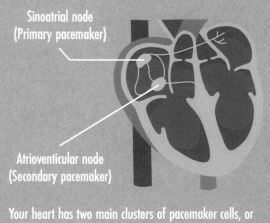

Sinoatrial node
(Primary pacemaker)

Atrioventicular node
(Secondary pacemaker)

Your heart has two main clusters of pacemaker cells, or cells with automaticity, which set the tempo for all heart cells to follow. The sinoatrial (or SA) node is the lead conductor, pulsing over 60 times a minute. If the SA node should ever slow down or fail, the atrioventricular (or AV) node is ready to step in, though it can only manage around 40 beats per minute.

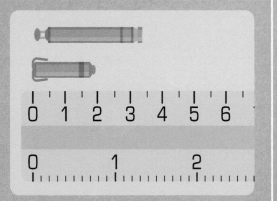

If a person's pacemaker cells lose rhythm or develop other issues, the person may be fitted with an artificial pacemaker, a device that sends electric signals to keep the heart beating. The smallest artificial pacemakers can fit inside a person's heart, and researchers are exploring whether transplanted pacemaker cells from humans or even animals could someday do the job.

I'm sure that's right. But my heart follows the beat of a salsa drum!

DOI: 10.4324/9781003292111-33

PECULIAR PLATELETS

When it comes to blood, red blood cells and white blood cells get most of the love. But if your blood ever comes out of you—and we hope it doesn't!—you'll want another type of blood cell backing you up: platelets.

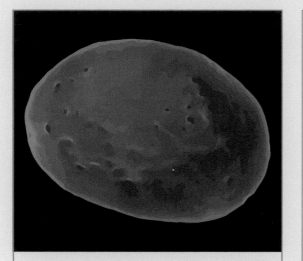

Platelets don't look like much, and they've got a name to match. Under the microscope, they look like plates, and they're small, so: platelets. It's possibly the least creative naming job in all of science. But platelets don't look like much for a reason: they're actually bits of larger cells. They have no nucleus or nuclear genes. But they do a lot with the little they have to work with.

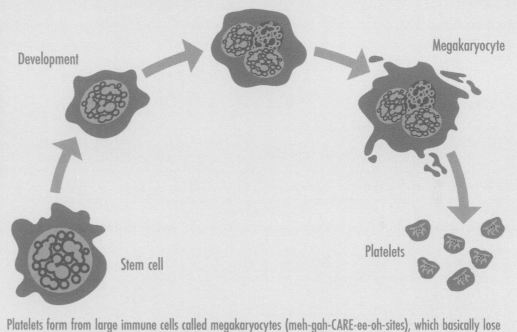

Development

Megakaryocyte

Stem cell

Platelets

Platelets form from large immune cells called megakaryocytes (meh-gah-CARE-ee-oh-sites), which basically lose their nucleus and shred the rest of themselves into confetti, producing thousands of platelets in the process. These platelets circulate in the blood for 8 to 10 days before breaking down, and our bodies create around 100 billion per day to keep up the supply.

The main role of platelets is to detect signs of blood vessel damage. When they do, they "activate"—sending out additional signals to recruit help to repair the break and spreading out in all directions like tiny Velcro koosh balls. The activated platelets clump together at the spot of the wound, forming a clot to seal the damaged vessel and prevent more bleeding.

I had no idea I was full of smart confetti!

DOI: 10.4324/9781003292111-34

35 LYMPH IS NO WIMP

Lymph. It sounds like a weird potion from a fantasy novel, but it's actually much cooler. Lymph is the main goop that oozes through the lymphatic system, which protects you from harm from dangerous invaders.

Lymph is clear fluid collected from body tissues. The lymphatic vessels carry this fluid to the bloodstream.

COMPOSITION OF LYMPH

- Glucose
- Bacteria
- Virus
- Salt
- Dead cells

96% Water

Lymphocytes (white blood cells that attack germs and produce antibodies.)

Clean lymph out

Dirty lymph in

Lymph node

Lymph nodes are like a car wash. The lymph enters dirty and full of germs. The lymphocytes inside the lymph nodes destroy the harmful germs and foreign bodies.

LIVER
Some people need to have their spleen surgically removed. For these people, the liver takes over most of the functions for the spleen.

Lymph nodes

SPLEEN

The spleen is the largest organ in the lymphatic system. The spleen acts a lot like a lymph node, but it cleans the blood.

ON THE MOVE...
Unlike the circulatory system, the lymphatic system does not have an organ like the heart to pump lymph. Instead, lymph relies on gravity and your muscle movements to move. Every time you take a walk, or even take a breath, you are moving around lymph.

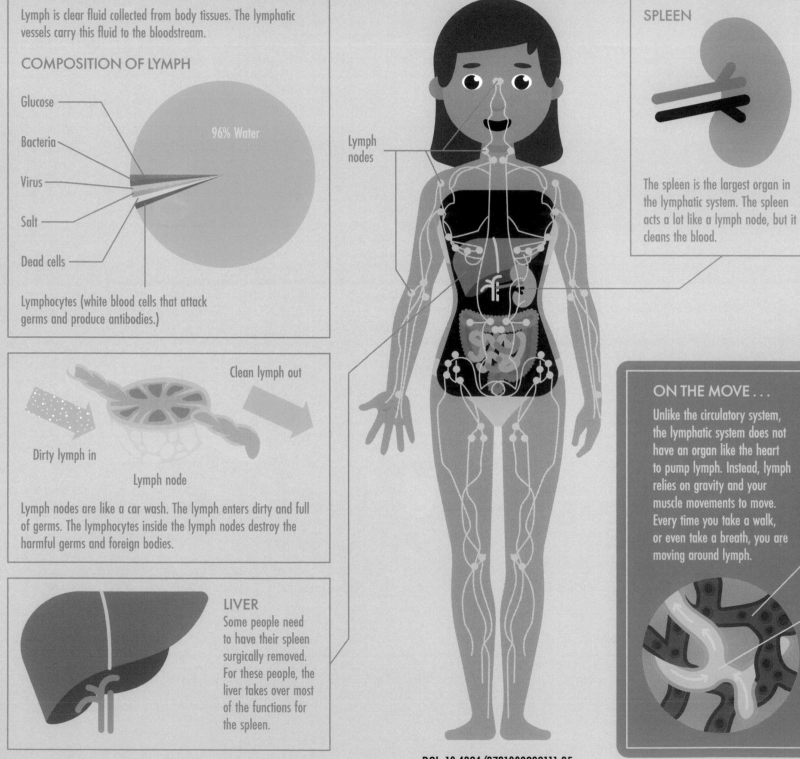

52

DOI: 10.4324/9781003292111-35

TONSILS

Tonsils produce lymphocytes and help to prevent germs from entering through the mouth and throat. Some people need to have their tonsils removed due to frequent throat infections.

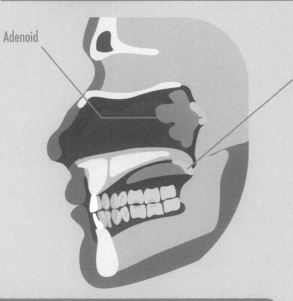

Adenoid

The movement of lymph throughout the body helps your body to maintain water balance. People who have had lymph nodes removed or a blockage of the lymph system can develop a condition called lymphedema, in which fluid from the tissues cannot drain properly into the lymphatic system.

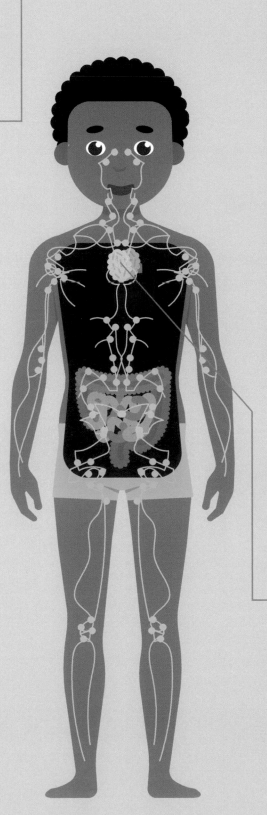

However, like veins, most lymphatic vessels have valves. These valves open and close to make sure lymph flows in the right direction.

Veins

Lymphatic vessels

Valves

THYMUS

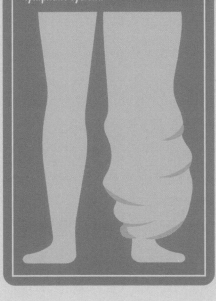

The thymus gets its name because it is shaped like a thyme leaf. The thymus is crucial to the development of lymphocytes in babies and young children. The thymus grows until adolescence and then starts to shrink in adulthood. By the time you are a grandparent, your thymus will be mostly replaced by fat!

36 CALL IN THE (IMMUNO) CAVALRY

Genetic mutations occur in our bodies' cells all the time. In most cases, mutations will weaken a cell due to an altered gene or protein that no longer works properly. Our immune systems are on constant lookout for cells that seem "wrong", and our bodies are extremely good at identifying and removing them to restore healthy function of our tissues and organs.

Occasionally, a mutation may have a different effect. If a mutation inactivates a gene that limits cell growth, for instance, the cell could rapidly grow and divide, and potentially become cancerous. Our immune system is also very good at removing these cells, usually—but some rogue cells find ways to fool or avoid the immune system and continue growing out of control.

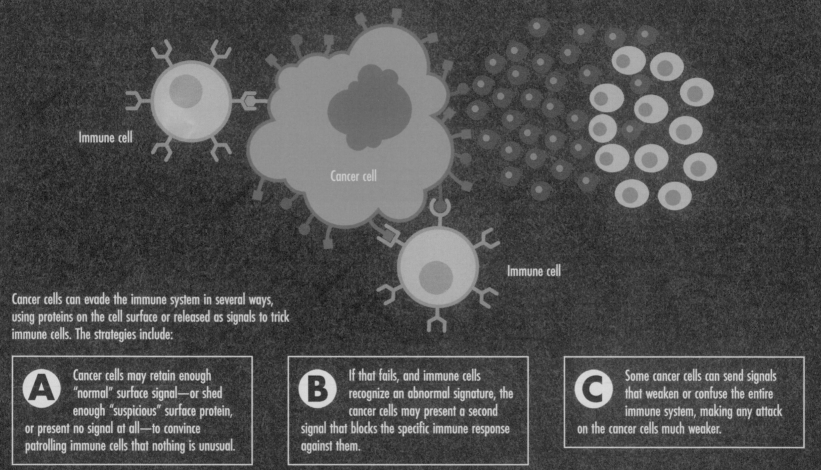

Immune cell

Cancer cell

Immune cell

Cancer cells can evade the immune system in several ways, using proteins on the cell surface or released as signals to trick immune cells. The strategies include:

A Cancer cells may retain enough "normal" surface signal—or shed enough "suspicious" surface protein, or present no signal at all—to convince patrolling immune cells that nothing is unusual.

B If that fails, and immune cells recognize an abnormal signature, the cancer cells may present a second signal that blocks the specific immune response against them.

C Some cancer cells can send signals that weaken or confuse the entire immune system, making any attack on the cancer cells much weaker.

In case you're wondering about that "second signal": basically, your immune system is a lean, mean cell-killing machine. Once activated and pointed at a target, immune cells are ruthlessly efficient in wiping it out of existence. A mistake in targeting—like attacking your own cells—is incredibly bad.

This type of self-attack is called autoimmune disease. To prevent it, some immune cells respond to signals called "checkpoints". If they're on the attack, preparing an attack, or peering squinty-eyed at something they'd very much like to attack, a checkpoint signal will stop the process. It's like a secret handshake, saying, "Wait, it's me! We're on the same team!" Some cancers, which are very much *not* on the right "team", find ways to send the same signals.

DOI: 10.4324/9781003292111-36

Fortunately, scientists are discovering ways to help immune systems see through cancer cells' trickery. Treatments based on this research are called "immunotherapy", because rather than battling cancer with drugs or radiation, they instead reinforce the body's immune system to get back on its feet and fight again. Here are a couple of ways that's being done today:

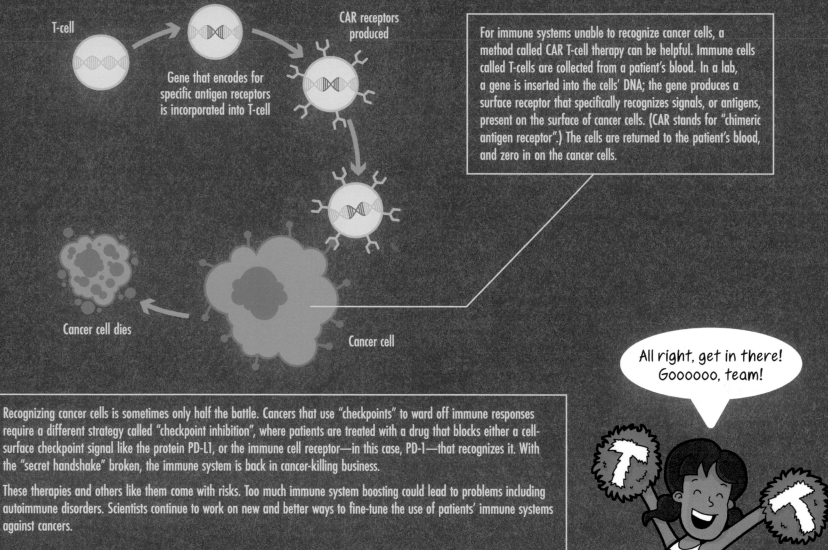

T-cell

Gene that encodes for specific antigen receptors is incorporated into T-cell

CAR receptors produced

For immune systems unable to recognize cancer cells, a method called CAR T-cell therapy can be helpful. Immune cells called T-cells are collected from a patient's blood. In a lab, a gene is inserted into the cells' DNA; the gene produces a surface receptor that specifically recognizes signals, or antigens, present on the surface of cancer cells. (CAR stands for "chimeric antigen receptor".) The cells are returned to the patient's blood, and zero in on the cancer cells.

Cancer cell dies

Cancer cell

All right, get in there! Goooooo, team!

Recognizing cancer cells is sometimes only half the battle. Cancers that use "checkpoints" to ward off immune responses require a different strategy called "checkpoint inhibition", where patients are treated with a drug that blocks either a cell-surface checkpoint signal like the protein PD-L1, or the immune cell receptor—in this case, PD-1—that recognizes it. With the "secret handshake" broken, the immune system is back in cancer-killing business.

These therapies and others like them come with risks. Too much immune system boosting could lead to problems including autoimmune disorders. Scientists continue to work on new and better ways to fine-tune the use of patients' immune systems against cancers.

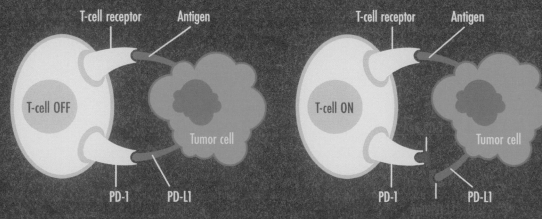

T-cell receptor   Antigen   T-cell receptor   Antigen

T-cell OFF   T-cell ON

Tumor cell   Tumor cell

PD-1   PD-L1   PD-1   PD-L1

55

FIGHT BACK WITH A VAC(CINE)

"Practice makes perfect." "Be prepared." "Keep your friends close, and your enemies closer." These can all be useful pieces of advice, and they're all mottos your immune system would love. Your immune cells spend your entire life keeping infections at bay, using a virtual "Most Wanted" list. Vaccines can help us help them to help us. Which helps them. And also us.

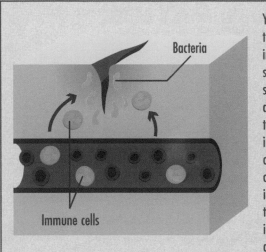

Bacteria

Immune cells

Your immune system has two parts. The first, the innate immune response, is stout and fast, but not very specific. It's more of a "you don't belong here" reaction to germs that try to sneak in. Including the skin and other barriers, patrolling cells on the lookout for intruders, and "killer" cells that destroy threats, innate immunity packs a wallop and reacts in minutes.

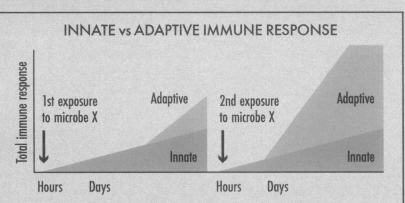

INNATE vs ADAPTIVE IMMUNE RESPONSE

Total immune response

1st exposure to microbe X — Adaptive — Innate

Hours — Days

2nd exposure to microbe X — Adaptive — Innate

Hours — Days

The other part of your immune system is the adaptive immune response and—true to the name—it "adapts" to specifically fight off pathogens it's already seen. This response is generally slower, but it's very specific and the "memory" of previous perpetrators can last for years. You think your Aunt Edith holds a grudge? She's got nothing on your adaptive immune system.

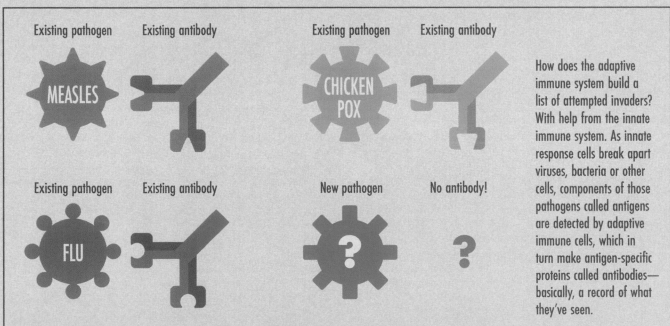

Existing pathogen — Existing antibody

MEASLES

Existing pathogen — Existing antibody

CHICKEN POX

Existing pathogen — Existing antibody

FLU

New pathogen — No antibody!

?   ?

How does the adaptive immune system build a list of attempted invaders? With help from the innate immune system. As innate response cells break apart viruses, bacteria or other cells, components of those pathogens called antigens are detected by adaptive immune cells, which in turn make antigen-specific proteins called antibodies— basically, a record of what they've seen.

Antibodies sit on the surface of adaptive immune cells, waiting for a repeat encounter with the one perfectly-fitting Cinderella antigen. If the antigen does show up again, the immune cell activates and divides into many cells, which release millions of antigen-locking antibodies into the bloodstream. The antibodies bind the antigen on the invaders, marking them for attack.

DOI: 10.4324/9781003292111-37

Where do vaccines fit into the picture? Vaccines are basically training camps for the adaptive immune system. Without vaccines, you must be infected by a germ for your body to produce antibodies specific for that threat. You may not want that, if the disease is highly contagious, hard to treat or recover from, or worms its way into you just before summer break.

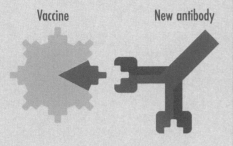

Vaccine   New antibody

Vaccines get the same job done, in a safer and more controlled way. Most vaccines are basically antigen stews—bits of dead germs, or germs that have been weakened or "attenuated", so they can't cause serious symptoms. Your innate immune system will clean up the mess—and in the process, help your adaptive immune system identify the germs, without an active infection.

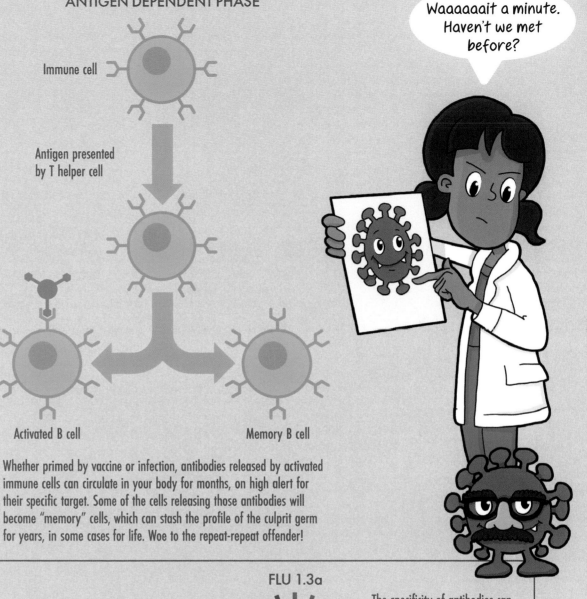

Immune cell

Antigen presented by T helper cell

Activated B cell   Memory B cell

Whether primed by vaccine or infection, antibodies released by activated immune cells can circulate in your body for months, on high alert for their specific target. Some of the cells releasing those antibodies will become "memory" cells, which can stash the profile of the culprit germ for years, in some cases for life. Woe to the repeat-repeat offender!

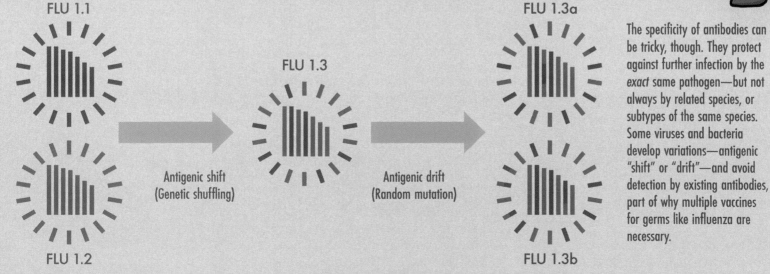

FLU 1.1

FLU 1.2

Antigenic shift (Genetic shuffling)

FLU 1.3

Antigenic drift (Random mutation)

FLU 1.3a

FLU 1.3b

The specificity of antibodies can be tricky, though. They protect against further infection by the *exact* same pathogen—but not always by related species, or subtypes of the same species. Some viruses and bacteria develop variations—antigenic "shift" or "drift"—and avoid detection by existing antibodies, part of why multiple vaccines for germs like influenza are necessary.

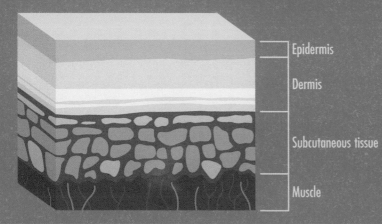

LAYERS OF HUMAN SKIN

Epidermis

Dermis

Subcutaneous tissue

Muscle

Nobody likes getting shots. But plenty of important treatments and vaccines come by way of the syringe, so we roll up our sleeves and (literally) take our medicine. But what if we could get some of those shots without the jab? Could a better alternative to one big needle be . . . hundreds of tiny ones?

You're really getting under my skin. So, thanks!

That's the idea behind microneedles, an idea first developed in the 1970s to get around the problem of skin. Many treatments could be applied topically, or onto the skin, rather than via syringe—but our skin has one main job, which is to keep things outside our body from getting in. With multiple layers and defenses, our skin slams the door on most topical treatments.

Up close, microneedles may look like something out of Dr. Frankenstein's hobby closet. But the "micro" part is key—the needles are large enough to penetrate skin, but too short to reach nerve endings or blood vessels underneath. So using them is painless. The needles can be coated or filled with medicine to deliver, and some will even dissolve following the treatment.

A recent twist on microneedles is called STAR particles. These tiny ceramic star-shaped particles are rubbed onto skin before applying a topical cream. The points of the STARs act like microneedles, piercing the outer skin and allowing better absorption by the body. It's like tenderizing a steak before a marinade, only you're the steak and the marinade is medicine. Tasty!

DOI: 10.4324/9781003292111-38

"BIG EATERS", BIG APPETITES

When you find trouble, there are lots of people you can call for help. Your parents. A teacher. Emergency services. Batman, if you have the right flashlight handy. But when your body finds trouble, it calls on a particular type of cell to save the day: macrophages.

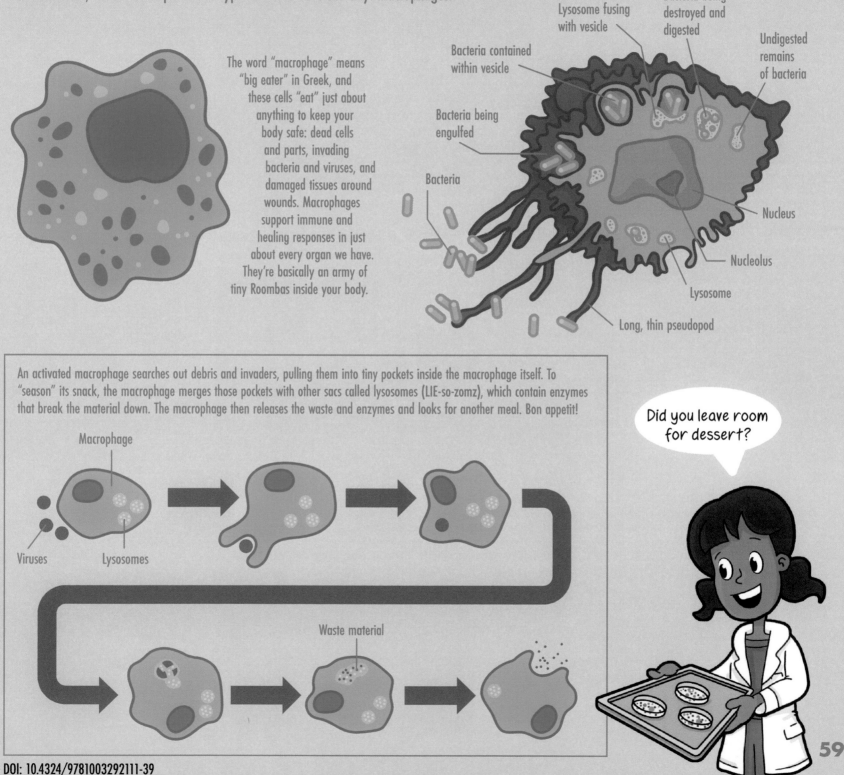

The word "macrophage" means "big eater" in Greek, and these cells "eat" just about anything to keep your body safe: dead cells and parts, invading bacteria and viruses, and damaged tissues around wounds. Macrophages support immune and healing responses in just about every organ we have. They're basically an army of tiny Roombas inside your body.

Lysosome fusing with vesicle

Bacteria being destroyed and digested

Bacteria contained within vesicle

Undigested remains of bacteria

Bacteria being engulfed

Bacteria

Nucleus

Nucleolus

Lysosome

Long, thin pseudopod

An activated macrophage searches out debris and invaders, pulling them into tiny pockets inside the macrophage itself. To "season" its snack, the macrophage merges those pockets with other sacs called lysosomes (LIE-so-zomz), which contain enzymes that break the material down. The macrophage then releases the waste and enzymes and looks for another meal. Bon appetit!

Macrophage

Viruses   Lysosomes

Waste material

Did you leave room for dessert?

DOI: 10.4324/9781003292111-39

EYES NEED SOME LASERS

How keen is your vision? Vision problems are common, especially as you age. In fact, only 35% of adults have perfect 20/20 vision without glasses or contact lenses. However, laser eye surgery can help correct not-so-perfect eyeballs.

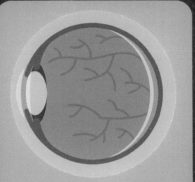

The shape of your eyeball, cornea, and lens affects how your eye processes light.

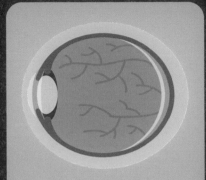

Nearsightedness occurs when a person can see things that are close by clearly, but things that are far away are blurry. Nearsightedness is often caused when an eye is too long, or the lens is too curved.

People with farsightedness can see far things clearly but close by objects are blurry. Farsightedness is caused when the eye is too short, or the lens has too little curve.

1 Laser eye surgery can correct these vision problems by changing the shape of the cornea to bounce light in the right direction. First, a numbing agent is applied to the eye.

2 A laser is used to cut a flap in the outer surface of the cornea.

3 Another laser is used to reshape the cornea.

4 The doctor closes the flap, and the person's vision is corrected!

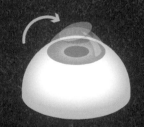

This is cool, but how do I get my eyes to shoot lasers?

DOI: 10.4324/9781003292111-40

BIBLIOGRAPHY

Germs Get Under (and On) Your Skin

"Viruses Live on Doorknobs and Phones and Can Get You Sick—Smart Cleaning and Good Habits Can Help Protect You - the Pursuit - University of Michigan School of Public Health." Sph.umich.edu, sph.umich.edu/pursuit/2020posts/smart-cleaning-for-viruses.html.

World Health Organization. "Normal Bacterial Flora on Hands." Nih.gov, World Health Organization, 2009, www.ncbi.nlm.nih.gov/books/NBK144001/.

Germopolis

"Bacteria on Your Skin Could Speed Healing." *Nature*, vol. 553, no. 7689, Jan. 2018, pp. 383–383, 10.1038/d41586-018-00960-3.

Crew, Bec. "Here's How Many Cells in Your Body Aren't Actually Human." *ScienceAlert*, 2018, www.sciencealert.com/how-many-bacteria-cells-outnumber-human-cells-microbiome-science.

Gibbons, Sean M., et al. "Ecological Succession and Viability of Human-Associated Microbiota on Restroom Surfaces." *Applied and Environmental Microbiology*, vol. 81, no. 2, 14 Nov. 2014, pp. 765–773, aem.asm.org/content/81/2/765, 10.1128/aem.03117-14.

Gilbert, Jack A. "Our Unique Microbial Identity." *Genome Biology*, vol. 16, no. 1, 14 May 2015, 10.1186/s13059-015-0664-7.

Koskinen, Kaisa, et al. "The Nasal Microbiome Mirrors and Potentially Shapes Olfactory Function." *Scientific Reports*, vol. 8, no. 1, 22 Jan. 2018, p. 1296, www.nature.com/articles/s41598-018-19438-3, 10.1038/s41598-018-19438-3.

"Mapping the Human Cell Atlas - Charting the Body's Cellular World." *Wellcome Sanger Institute Blog*, 8 Apr. 2020, sangerinstitute.blog/2020/04/08/mapping-the-human-cell-atlas-charting-the-bodys-cellular-world/.

"NIH Human Microbiome Project Defines Normal Bacterial Makeup of the Body." *National Institutes of Health (NIH)*, 31 Aug. 2015, www.nih.gov/news-events/news-releases/nih-human-microbiome-project-defines-normal-bacterial-makeup-body#:~:text=The%20human%20body%20contains%20trillions.

Raveh-Sadka, Tali, et al. "Gut Bacteria Are Rarely Shared by Co-Hospitalized Premature Infants, regardless of Necrotizing Enterocolitis Development." *ELife*, vol. 4, 3 Mar. 2015, www.ncbi.nlm.nih.gov/pmc/articles/PMC4384745/pdf/elife05477.pdf, 10.7554/elife.05477.

Many More Microbiomes

Am, et al. "These Bacteria Have Adapted to Life in Your Nose—and That May Be Good News." *Science | AAAS*, 27 May 2020, www.sciencemag.org/news/2020/05/these-bacteria-have-adapted-life-your-nose-and-may-be-good-news.

"Bacteria in Lungs: New Lung Microbiome Study Shows How They Get There." *University of Michigan*, labblog.uofmhealth.org/lab-report/bacteria-your-lungs-new-microbiome-study-shows-how-they-get-there.

Beck, James M., et al. "The Microbiome of the Lung." *Translational Research : The Journal of Laboratory and Clinical Medicine*, vol. 160, no. 4, 1 Oct. 2012, pp. 258–266, www.ncbi.nlm.nih.gov/pmc/articles/PMC3440512/, 10.1016/j.trsl.2012.02.005.

Davenport, Francesca, et al. "Natural Lung Bacteria Offer Clues on Treating Airway Infections, Says Expert." *Medicalxpress.com*, medicalxpress.com/news/2018-01-natural-lung-bacteria-clues-airway.html. Accessed 17 Jan. 2022.

Hulcr, Jiri, et al. "A Jungle in There: Bacteria in Belly Buttons Are Highly Diverse, but Predictable." *PLoS ONE*, vol. 7, no. 11, 7 Nov. 2012, p. e47712, 10.1371/journal.pone.0047712. Accessed 8 July 2021.

Koskinen, Kaisa, et al. "The Nasal Microbiome Mirrors and Potentially Shapes Olfactory Function." *Scientific Reports*, vol. 8, no. 1, 22 Jan. 2018, p. 1296, www.nature.com/articles/s41598-018-19438-3, 10.1038/s41598-018-19438-3.

Mass, Mark B. Abelson, MD, CM, DSc, FRCSC, FARVO, Keith Lane, and Connie Slocum, PhD, Andover. "The Secrets of Ocular Microbiomes." *www.reviewofophthalmology.com*, www.reviewofophthalmology.com/article/the-secrets-of-ocular-microbiomes. Accessed 17 Jan. 2022.

"Microbiome Monday: The Ecosystem in Your Belly Button | AMNH." *American Museum of Natural History*, 2015, www.amnh.org/explore/news-blogs/news-posts/microbiome-monday-the-ecosystem-in-your-belly-button.

"Microbiome of the Eye." *American Academy of Ophthalmology*, 29 Jan. 2019, www.aao.org/eye-health/anatomy/microbiome-of-eye.

Nield, David. "Your Nose Has Its Own Microbiome, and It Might Be Possible to Change It, Study Shows." *ScienceAlert*, www.sciencealert.com/your-nose-bacteria-might-play-a-role-in-good-health-just-like-the-gut-microbiome. Accessed 17 Jan. 2022.

US, Tony St Leger, The Conversation. "Meet the Eye Microbiome." *Scientific American*, www.scientificamerican.com/article/meet-the-eye-microbiome/.

"What Lives in Your Belly Button? Study Finds 'Rain Forest' of Species." *Nationalgeographic.com*, 14 Nov. 2012, www.nationalgeographic.com/news/2012/11/121114-belly-button-bacteria-science-health-dunn/.

It Takes Guts to Be This Germy

"How Bacteria in Your Gut Interact with the Mind and Body." *www.heart.org*, www.heart.org/en/news/2020/05/28/how-bacteria-in-your-gut-interact-with-the-mind-and-body.

Inman, Mason. "How Bacteria Turn Fiber into Food." *PLoS Biology*, vol. 9, no. 12, 20 Dec. 2011, p. e1001227, www.ncbi.nlm.nih.gov/pmc/articles/PMC3243711/, 10.1371/journal.pbio.1001227.

Publishing, Harvard Health. "Can Gut Bacteria Improve Your Health?" *Harvard Health*, www.health.harvard.edu/staying-healthy/can-gut-bacteria-improve-your-health#:~:text=Your%20gut%20microbiota%20plays%20many.

Balancing Your Gut Bacteria Like a Pro (or a Pre!)

Mach, Núria, and Dolors Fuster-Botella. "Endurance Exercise and Gut Microbiota: A Review." *Journal of Sport and Health Science*, vol. 6, no. 2, June 2017, pp. 179–197, www.sciencedirect.com/science/article/pii/S2095254616300163, 10.1016/j.jshs.2016.05.001.

"Prebiotics and Probiotics Creating a Healthier You." *Eatright.org*, 2018, www.eatright.org/food/vitamins-and-supplements/nutrient-rich-foods/prebiotics-and-probiotics-creating-a-healthier-you.

"Prebiotics vs. Probiotics: What's the Difference?" *Health Essentials from Cleveland Clinic*, 25 Mar. 2020, health.clevelandclinic.org/prebiotics-vs-probiotics-whats-the-difference/.

"Probiotics and Prebiotics: What You Should Know." *Mayo Clinic*, 2018, www.mayoclinic.org/healthy-lifestyle/consumer-health/expert-answers/probiotics/faq-20058065.

Bring Back My Biome to Me

D'Haens, Geert R., and Christian Jobin. "Fecal Microbial Transplantation for Diseases beyond Recurrent Clostridium Difficile Infection." *Gastroenterology*, vol. 157, no. 3, 1 Sept. 2019, pp. 624–636, www.gastrojournal.org/article/S0016-5085(19)41017-2/fulltext, 10.1053/j.gastro.2019.04.053. Accessed 17 Jan. 2022.

"Fecal Transplant: An Old Remedy Made New - Advances in Gastroenterology and GI Surgery | NewYork-Presbyterian." *www.nyp.org*, www.nyp.org/advances-gastroenterology/fecal-transplant-an-old-remedy-made-new. Accessed 17 Jan. 2022.

Jo Ann Day. "Fecal Transplantation (Bacteriotherapy) | Johns Hopkins Division of Gastroenterology and Hepatology." *Hopkinsmedicine.org*, 26 Apr. 2017, www.hopkinsmedicine.org/gastroenterology_hepatology/clinical_services/advanced_endoscopy/fecal_transplantation.html.

Wilson, Brooke C., et al. "The Super-Donor Phenomenon in Fecal Microbiota Transplantation." *Frontiers in Cellular and Infection Microbiology*, vol. 9, 21 Jan. 2019, www.frontiersin.org/articles/10.3389/fcimb.2019.00002/full, 10.3389/fcimb.2019.00002.

Let's Have Some Fun(gi)

Cui, Lijia, et al. "The Human Mycobiome in Health and Disease." *Genome Medicine*, vol. 5, no. 7, 2013, p. 63, 10.1186/gm467. Accessed 29 July 2019.

Huseyin, Chloe E., et al. "Forgotten Fungi—the Gut Mycobiome in Human Health and Disease." *FEMS Microbiology Reviews*, vol. 41, no. 4, 18 Apr. 2017, pp. 479–511, 10.1093/femsre/fuw047. Accessed 8 Mar. 2021.

Seed, P. C. "The Human Mycobiome." *Cold Spring Harbor Perspectives in Medicine*, vol. 5, no. 5, 10 Nov. 2014, pp. a019810–a019810, perspectivesinmedicine.cshlp.org/content/5/5/a019810.full, 10.1101/cshperspect.a019810. Accessed 24 Sept. 2019.

Ward, Tonya L., et al. "Development of the Human Mycobiome over the First Month of Life and across Body Sites." *MSystems*, 6 Mar. 2018, msystems.asm.org/content/3/3/e00140-17, 10.1128/mSystems.00140-17. Accessed 17 Jan. 2022.

Mite You Spare a Follicle?

"3 Things You Didn't Know about the Mites That Live on Your Face." *Discover Magazine*, www.discovermagazine.com/planet-earth/3-things-you-didnt-know-about-the-mites-that-live-on-your-face.

"Causes of Rosacea: Demodex Mites & Microbes." *Rosacea.org*, www.rosacea.org/patients/causes-of-rosacea/demodex-mites-and-microbes.

"Demodex - an Overview | ScienceDirect Topics." *www.sciencedirect.com*, www.sciencedirect.com/topics/biochemistry-genetics-and-molecular-biology/demodex.

Derr, Erik. "Mite-O-Rama: Whole Colonies of Tiny Creatures Live on Your Face." *Latin Post - Latin News, Immigration, Politics, Culture*, 1 Sept. 2014, www.latinpost.com/articles/20473/20140901/mite-o-rama-whole-colonies-of-tiny-creatures-live-on-our-faces.htm. Accessed 17 Jan. 2022.

Handwerk, Brian. "Your Hair Mites Are so Loyal Their DNA Reflects Your Ancestry." *Smithsonian Magazine*, www.smithsonianmag.com/science-nature/your-hair-mites-are-so-loyal-their-dna-reflects-your-ancestry-180957545/.

"Hundreds of Tiny Arachnids Are Likely on Your Face Right Now." *Magazine*, 23 Apr. 2020, www.nationalgeographic.com/magazine/2020/05/face-mites-the-tiny-tenants-that-likely-live-in-your-pores/. Accessed 17 Jan. 2022.

Jones, Lucy. "These Microscopic Mites Live on Your Face." *Bbc.com*, 2015, www.bbc.com/earth/story/20150508-these-mites-live-on-your-face.

Rather, ParvaizAnwar, and Iffat Hassan. "Human Demodex Mite: The Versatile Mite of Dermatological Importance." *Indian Journal of Dermatology*, vol. 59, no. 1, 2014, p. 60, www.ncbi.nlm.nih.gov/pmc/articles/PMC3884930/, 10.4103/0019-5154.123498.

"Rosacea: Who Gets and Causes." *www.aad.org*, www.aad.org/public/diseases/rosacea/what-is/causes.

Ah-CHOO! It's Dust Mitey in Here

"Dust Mite Allergy - Symptoms and Causes." *Mayo Clinic*, 2019, www.mayoclinic.org/diseases-conditions/dust-mites/symptoms-causes/syc-20352173.

"Dust Mites." *www.lung.org*, www.lung.org/clean-air/at-home/indoor-air-pollutants/dust-mites#:~:text=Reduce%20humidity.. Accessed 17 Jan. 2022.

"Dust Mites and Cockroaches." *National Institute of Environmental Health Sciences*, www.niehs.nih.gov/health/topics/agents/allergens/dustmites/index.cfm.

"Patients & Families | UW Health." *Patient.uwhealth.org*, www.uwhealth.org/healthfacts/allergy/6180.pdf. Accessed 17 Jan. 2022.

Services, AAFA Community. "Fact or Fiction: 5 Myths about Dust Mites." *Asthma and Allergy Foundation of America*, community.aafa.org/blog/fact-or-fiction-5-myths-about-dust-mites. Accessed 17 Jan. 2022.

"Tracing the Chemistry of Household Dust." *Acs.org*, 2021, cen.acs.org/articles/95/i7/Tracing-chemistry-household-dust.html#:~:text=More%20than%20just%20dirt%2C%20house.

Beds, Bugs and Beyond

"Bedbugs Evolved More than 100 Million Years Ago." *ScienceDaily*, www.sciencedaily.com/releases/2019/05/190516114607.htm.

"Learning from Lice | Accumulating Glitches | Learn Science at Scitable." *www.nature.com*, www.nature.com/scitable/blog/accumulating-glitches/learning_from_lice/. Accessed 17 Jan. 2022.

Toups, M. A., et al. "Origin of Clothing Lice Indicates Early Clothing Use by Anatomically Modern Humans in Africa." *Molecular Biology and Evolution*, vol. 28, no. 1, 7 Sept. 2010, pp. 29–32, 10.1093/molbev/msq234.

We Are an Island: The Evolution of Human Parasite Species - Understanding Evolution. 1 Mar. 2015, evolution.berkeley.edu/evolibrary/news/150309_bedbugs. Accessed 17 Jan. 2022.

"What the Bugs That Live on Our Bodies Say about Human History." *Discover Magazine*, www.discovermagazine.com/planet-earth/what-the-bugs-that-live-on-our-bodies-say-about-human-history.

Incredibly Crafty Critters

Berthold, Emma. "The Link between Cats, Your Brain and Your Behaviour." *Curious*, 28 Aug. 2018, www.science.org.au/curious/people-medicine/link-between-cats-your-brain-and-your-behaviour.

Bucklin, Stephanie. "7 Strange Facts about the 'Mind-Control' Parasite Toxoplasma Gondii." *Livescience.com*, Live Science, 18 Oct. 2016, www.livescience.com/56529-strange-facts-about-toxoplasma-gondii-parasite.html.

Flegr, Jaroslav, et al. "Fatal Attraction Phenomenon in Humans – Cat Odour Attractiveness Increased for Toxoplasma-Infected Men While Decreased for Infected Women." *PLoS Neglected Tropical Diseases*, vol. 5, no. 11, 8 Nov. 2011, p. e1389, 10.1371/journal.pntd.0001389. Accessed 18 Jan. 2021.

Lanese, Nicoletta. "What Is Toxoplasmosis?" *Livescience.com*, 27 Jan. 2020, www.livescience.com/toxoplasmosis.html. Accessed 17 Jan. 2022.

Vyas, A., et al. "Behavioral Changes Induced by Toxoplasma Infection of Rodents Are Highly Specific to Aversion of Cat Odors." *Proceedings of the National Academy of Sciences*, vol. 104, no. 15, 2 Apr. 2007, pp. 6442–6447, www.pnas.org/content/104/15/6442, 10.1073/pnas.0608310104.

I Spy, Inside My Little Eye...

"Floaters | National Eye Institute." *www.nei.nih.gov*, www.nei.nih.gov/learn-about-eye-health/eye-conditions-and-diseases/floaters.

Proctor, Jason G. Goldman / Illustration by Adam. "Why Do You Get 'Eye Floaters'?" *www.bbc.com*, www.bbc.com/future/article/20160113-why-do-you-get-eye-floaters. Accessed 17 Jan. 2022.

Skerrett, Patrick J. "What You Can Do about Floaters and Flashes in the Eye - Harvard Health Blog." *Harvard Health Blog*, 10 June 2013, www.health.harvard.edu/blog/what-you-can-do-about-floaters-and-flashes-in-the-eye-201306106336.

Webb, Blake F., et al. "Prevalence of Vitreous Floaters in a Community Sample of Smartphone Users." *International Journal of Ophthalmology*, vol. 6, no. 3, 18 June 2013, pp. 402–405, www.ncbi.nlm.nih.gov/pmc/articles/PMC3693028/, 10.3980/j.issn.2222-3959.2013.03.27. Accessed 16 June 2021.

Microbes to the Rescue

Hoffman, Robert M. "Bugging Tumors: Figure 1." *Cancer Discovery*, vol. 2, no. 7, July 2012, pp. 588–590, 10.1158/2159-8290.cd-12-0227. Accessed 1 Jan. 2020.

"How Did They Make Penicillin?" *Nih.gov*, 2019, www.nlm.nih.gov/exhibition/fromdnatobeer/exhibition-interactive/illustrations/penicillin-alternative.html.

"How Tiny, Microbe-Propelled Bots Could Deliver Drugs in Our Bodies." *Smithsonian Magazine*, www.smithsonianmag.com/innovation/how-tiny-microbe-propelled-bots-could-deliver-drugs-in-our-bodies-180973211/.

"Microbial Physicians: Delivering Drugs with Bacteria." *Science in the News*, 17 Mar. 2017, sitn.hms.harvard.edu/flash/2017/microbial-physicians-delivering-drugs-bacteria/. Accessed 17 Jan. 2022.

We All Go Viral

"Human Gut Virome Is Stable and Person-Specific." *The Scientist Magazine®*, www.the-scientist.com/news-opinion/human-gut-virome-is-stable-and-person-specific-66553. Accessed 17 Jan. 2022.

"Infographic: Human Endogenous Retroviruses and Disease." *The Scientist Magazine®*, www.the-scientist.com/infographics/infographic-65262. Accessed 17 Jan. 2022.

"Meet the Trillions of Viruses That Make up Your Virome | EarthSky.org." *Earthsky.org*, earthsky.org/human-world/trillions-of-viruses-human-virome.

"Our Complicated Relationship with Viruses." *ScienceDaily*, www.sciencedaily.com/releases/2016/11/161128151050.htm.

Pearce, Rebecca. "The Viral Content of Human Genomes Is More Variable than We Thought." *On Biology*, 25 Jan. 2019, blogs.biomedcentral.com/on-biology/2019/01/25/viral-content-human-genomes-variable-thought/. Accessed 17 Jan. 2022.

Pride, David. "Viruses Can Help Us as Well as Harm Us." *Scientific American*, Dec. 2020, www.scientificamerican.com/article/viruses-can-help-us-as-well-as-harm-us/, 10.1038/scientificamerican1220-46.

Shkoporov, Andrey N., et al. "The Human Gut Virome Is Highly Diverse, Stable, and Individual Specific." *Cell Host & Microbe*, vol. 26, no. 4, Oct. 2019, pp. 527-541.e5, 10.1016/j.chom.2019.09.009. Accessed 10 June 2020.

"The Influence of LINE-1 and SINE Retrotransposons on Mammalian Genomes." *Mobile DNA III*, 2019, pp. 1165–1208, www.ncbi.nlm.nih.gov/pmc/articles/PMC4498412/, 10.1128/microbiolspec.mdna3-0061-2014. Accessed 12 Dec. 2019.

"The Non-Human Living inside of You." *Cold Spring Harbor Laboratory*, 9 Jan. 2020, www.cshl.edu/the-non-human-living-inside-of-you/.

If You Can't Beat 'Em, Swallow 'Em Whole

Aanen, Duur K., and Paul Eggleton. "Symbiogenesis: Beyond the Endosymbiosis Theory?" *Journal of Theoretical Biology*, vol. 434, Dec. 2017, pp. 99–103, 10.1016/j.jtbi.2017.08.001.

Cooper, Geoffrey M. "The Origin and Evolution of Cells." *Nih.gov*, Sinauer Associates, 2000, www.ncbi.nlm.nih.gov/books/NBK9841/.

"From Prokaryotes to Eukaryotes." *Berkeley.edu*, 2019, evolution.berkeley.edu/evolibrary/article/_0/endosymbiosis_03.

kazilek. "Endosymbiotic Theory | Ask a Biologist." *Asu.edu*, 24 Feb. 2016, askabiologist.asu.edu/explore/cells-living-in-cells.

Poole, Anthony, and David Penny. "Does Endo-Symbiosis Explain the Origin of the Nucleus?" *Nature Cell Biology*, vol. 3, no. 8, Aug. 2001, pp. E173–E173, 10.1038/35087102.

Put Away That DNA!

Alberts, Bruce, et al. "Chromosomal DNA and Its Packaging in the Chromatin Fiber." *Nih.gov*, Garland Science, 2015, www.ncbi.nlm.nih.gov/books/NBK26834/.

Austin, Christopher. "Chromatin." *Genome.gov*, 2019, www.genome.gov/genetics-glossary/Chromatin.

"Chromatin | Learn Science at Scitable." *Nature.com*, 2014, www.nature.com/scitable/definition/chromatin-182/.

Cooper, Geoffrey M. "Chromosomes and Chromatin." *Nih.gov*, Sinauer Associates, 2019, www.ncbi.nlm.nih.gov/books/NBK9863/.

Margueron, Raphaël, and Danny Reinberg. "Chromatin Structure and the Inheritance of Epigenetic Information." *Nature Reviews Genetics*, vol. 11, no. 4, Apr. 2010, pp. 285–296, 10.1038/nrg2752.

Family Reunions are Bananas (Literally)

Carey, Bjorn. "Stanford Scientists Sequence Genome of Human's Closest Invertebrate Relative." *Stanford University*, 14 Aug. 2013, news.stanford.edu/news/2013/august/tunicate-genome-sequence-081413.html. Accessed 17 Jan. 2022.

"Comparative Genomics Fact Sheet." *Genome.gov*, 2015, www.genome.gov/about-genomics/fact-sheets/Comparative-Genomics-Fact-Sheet.

Cummins, Eleanor. "Humans Are Genetically Linked to Bananas." *Popular Science*, Popular Science, 14 Aug. 2018, www.popsci.com/humans-genetically-linked-to-bananas/.

"Fig. 19 Hox Genes in Mouse and Human with Their Phylogenetic..." *ResearchGate*, www.researchgate.net/figure/Hox-genes-in-mouse-and-human-with-their-phylogenetic-counterparts-in-Drosophila-39-Hox_fig9_49717129. Accessed 17 Jan. 2022.

Hardison, R. "Hemoglobins from Bacteria to Man: Evolution of Different Patterns of Gene Expression." *Journal of Experimental Biology*, vol. 201, no. 8, 1 Apr. 1998, pp. 1099–1117, 10.1242/jeb.201.8.1099. Accessed 8 Dec. 2021.

"Hox Genes." *Berkeley.edu*, 2019, evolution.berkeley.edu/evolibrary/article/side_0_0/hoxgenes_01.

"People Aren't Bananas | New Scientist." *www.newscientist.com*, www.newscientist.com/letter/mg17523584-000-people-arent-bananas/.

"Researchers Compare Chicken, Human Genomes." *Genome.gov*, www.genome.gov/12514316/2004-release-researchers-compare-chicken-human-genomes#:~:text=About%20 60%20percent%20of%20chicken.

Too Much of a Good Gene?

Collins, Dr Francis. "Gene Duplication: New Analysis Shows How Extra Copies Split the Work." *NIH Director's Blog*, 31 May 2016, directorsblog.nih.gov/2016/05/31/gene-duplication-new-analysis-shows-how-extra-copies-split-the-work/. Accessed 17 Jan. 2022.

"Origins of New Genes and Pseudogenes | Learn Science at Scitable." *www.nature.com*, www.nature.com/scitable/topicpage/origins-of-new-genes-and-pseudogenes-835/.

"Transposons: Your DNA That's on the Go." *Science in the News*, 26 Sept. 2018, sitn.hms.harvard.edu/flash/2018/transposons-your-dna-thats-on-the-go/.

Tutar, Yusuf. "Pseudogenes." *Comparative and Functional Genomics*, vol. 2012, 2012, pp. 1–4, www.ncbi.nlm.nih.gov/pmc/articles/PMC3352212/, 10.1155/2012/424526.

Zhang, Z. "Millions of Years of Evolution Preserved: A Comprehensive Catalog of the Processed Pseudogenes in the Human Genome." *Genome Research*, vol. 13, no. 12, 1 Dec. 2003, pp. 2541–2558, 10.1101/gr.1429003. Accessed 5 Dec. 2019.

Hox Rocks!

"Fig. 19 Hox Genes in Mouse and Human with Their Phylogenetic..." *ResearchGate*, www.researchgate.net/figure/Hox-genes-in-mouse-and-human-with-their-phylogenetic-counterparts-in-Drosophila-39-Hox_fig9_49717129.

"Hox Genes." *Berkeley.edu*, 2019, evolution.berkeley.edu/evolibrary/article/side_0_0/hoxgenes_01.

Balanced on the Hedge

Murphy, John. "How Sonic the Hedgehog Became a Cancer Fighter." *Mdlinx.com*, 2018, www.mdlinx.com/article/how-sonic-the-hedgehog-became-a-cancer-fighter/lfc-1725. Accessed 17 Jan. 2022.

Sasai, Noriaki, et al. "Hedgehog Signal and Genetic Disorders." *Frontiers in Genetics*, vol. 10, 8 Nov. 2019, www.ncbi.nlm.nih.gov/pmc/articles/PMC6856222/, 10.3389/fgene.2019.01103.

"SHH Gene: MedlinePlus Genetics." *Medlineplus.gov*, medlineplus.gov/genetics/gene/shh/#name. Accessed 17 Jan. 2022.

Telo Me Your Life Story

"Are Telomeres the Key to Aging and Cancer." *Utah.edu*, 2012, learn.genetics.utah.edu/content/basics/telomeres/.

emma.berthold@science.org.au. "What Are Telomeres?" *Curious*, 10 Oct. 2018, www.science.org.au/curious/people-medicine/what-are-telomeres.

McRae, Mike. "In a First, Scientists Say They've Partially Reversed a Cellular Aging Process in Humans." *ScienceAlert*, www.sciencealert.com/oxygen-therapy-found-to-turn-back-the-sands-of-time-on-our-body-s-aging-cells.

Shammas, Masood A. "Telomeres, Lifestyle, Cancer, and Aging." *Current Opinion in Clinical Nutrition and Metabolic Care*, vol. 14, no. 1, Jan. 2011, pp. 28–34, 10.1097/mco.0b013e32834121b1.

Whittemore, Kurt, et al. "Telomere Shortening Rate Predicts Species Life Span." *Proceedings of the National Academy of Sciences*, vol. 116, no. 30, 8 July 2019, pp. 15122–15127, www.pnas.org/content/116/30/15122, 10.1073/pnas.1902452116.

Just Here to Interfere

Hammond, Scott M. "An Overview of MicroRNAs." *Advanced Drug Delivery Reviews*, vol. 87, 29 June 2015, pp. 3–14, www.ncbi.nlm.nih.gov/pmc/articles/PMC4504744/, 10.1016/j.addr.2015.05.001. Accessed 28 May 2020.

"How RNAi Works - RNAi Biology | UMass Medical School." *University of Massachusetts Medical School*, 3 Nov. 2013, www.umassmed.edu/rti/biology/how-rnai-works/.

Lam, Jenny K W, et al. "SiRNA versus MiRNA as Therapeutics for Gene Silencing." *Molecular Therapy - Nucleic Acids*, vol. 4, 2015, p. e252, 10.1038/mtna.2015.23.

Mocellin, Simone, and Maurizio Provenzano. "RNA Interference: Learning Gene Knock-down from Cell Physiology." *Journal of Translational Medicine*, vol. 2, no. 1, 2004, p. 39, 10.1186/1479-5876-2-39.

National Human Genome Research Institute. "Human Genome Project FAQ." *Genome.gov*, 2013, www.genome.gov/human-genome-project/Completion-FAQ.

When Your Honker is Honking

Works Cited

Hasegawa, M., and E. B. Kern. "The Human Nasal Cycle." *Mayo Clinic Proceedings*, vol. 52, no. 1, 1 Jan. 1977, pp. 28–34, pubmed.ncbi.nlm.nih.gov/609283/. Accessed 17 Jan. 2022.

Hrala, Josh. "Here's the Frustrating Reason Only One Side of Your Nose Gets Blocked at a Time." *ScienceAlert*, www.sciencealert.com/why-does-your-nose-get-stuffy-only-one-side-at-a-time.

Kahana-Zweig, Roni, et al. "Measuring and Characterizing the Human Nasal Cycle." *PLOS ONE*, vol. 11, no. 10, 6 Oct. 2016, p. e0162918, 10.1371/journal.pone.0162918.

Noam, Sobel, et al. *Olfaction - the World Smells Different to Each Nostril.* Nature, Dec. 1999, www.researchgate.net/publication/12728657_Olfaction_-_The_world_smells_different_to_each_nostril.

"What Is the Nasal Cycle? | ENT and Sinus Center Corpus Christi, Tx." *www.ccentsinus.com*, www.ccentsinus.com/blog-nasal-cycle.html. Accessed 17 Jan. 2022.

Ugh, Brain Freeze!

"How to Ease Brain Freeze." *www.hopkinsmedicine.org*, www.hopkinsmedicine.org/health/conditions-and-diseases/how-to-ease-brain-freeze#:~:text=Brain%20freeze%2C%20otherwise%20known%20as. Accessed 17 Jan. 2022.

"What Causes Brain Freeze?" *www.houstonmethodist.org*, www.houstonmethodist.org/blog/articles/2020/jun/what-causes-brain-freeze/#:~:text=In%20this%20case%2C%20although%20it. Accessed 17 Jan. 2022.

"What Causes Brain Freeze? - Featured, Health Topics, Neuroscience." *Hackensack Meridian Health*, 21 Aug. 2020, www.hackensackmeridianhealth.org/HealthU/2020/08/21/what-causes-brain-freeze/#:~:text=Brain%20freeze%2C%20often%20referred%20to.

Nerves Made for Speed

Works Cited

"How Fast Can an Arrow Travel? — Soar Valley Archers." *Soar Valley Archers*, www.soarvalleyarchers.com/faqs/how-fast-can-an-arrow-travel/#:~:text=The%20faster%20an%20arrow%20travels. Accessed 17 Jan. 2022.

"Neuroscience for Kids - Conduction Velocity." *Faculty.washington.edu*, faculty.washington.edu/chudler/cv.html.

"Numbers: The Nervous System, from 268-MPH Signals to Trillions of Synapses." *Discover Magazine*, www.discovermagazine.com/health/numbers-the-nervous-system-from-268-mph-signals-to-trillions-of-synapses.

Purves, Dale, et al. "Increased Conduction Velocity as a Result of Myelination." *Neuroscience. 2nd Edition*, 2001, www.ncbi.nlm.nih.gov/books/NBK10921/#:~:text=By%20acting%20as%20an%20electrical.

---. "Increased Conduction Velocity as a Result of Myelination." *Neuroscience. 2nd Edition*, 2001, www.ncbi.nlm.nih.gov/books/NBK10921/#:~:text=By%20acting%20as%20an%20electrical.

Susuki, Keiichiro. "Myelin, Membrane | Learn Science at Scitable." *Nature.com*, 2010, www.nature.com/scitable/topicpage/myelin-a-specialized-membrane-for-cell-communication-14367205/.

"UCSB Science Line: How Fast Can Neurons Transmit through Your Body for the Nervous System to Function?" *Scienceline.ucsb.edu*, scienceline.ucsb.edu/getkey.php?key=5607#:~:text=Muscle%20command%20neurons%20have%20one. Accessed 17 Jan. 2022.

Human See, Human Do

Acharya, Sourya, and Samarth Shukla. "Mirror Neurons: Enigma of the Metaphysical Modular Brain." *Journal of Natural Science, Biology and Medicine*, vol. 3, no. 2, 2012, p. 118, www.ncbi.nlm.nih.gov/pmc/articles/PMC3510904/, 10.4103/0976-9668.101878.

"I Yawn, You Yawn, We All Yawn! | Riddles." *Sites.psu.edu*, sites.psu.edu/riddhipatel/2015/03/26/i-yawn-you-yawn-we-all-yawn/. Accessed 17 Jan. 2022.

Miller, G. "NEUROSCIENCE: Mirror Neurons May Help Songbirds Stay in Tune." *Science*, vol. 319, no. 5861, 18 Jan. 2008, pp. 269a269a, 10.1126/science.319.5861.269a. Accessed 8 Aug. 2019.

"Mirror Neuron System - an Overview | ScienceDirect Topics." *www.sciencedirect.com*, www.sciencedirect.com/topics/psychology/mirror-neuron-system.

Prochazkova, Eliska, and Mariska E. Kret. "Connecting Minds and Sharing Emotions through Mimicry: A Neurocognitive Model of Emotional Contagion." *Neuroscience & Biobehavioral Reviews*, vol. 80, Sept. 2017, pp. 99–114, 10.1016/j.neubiorev.2017.05.013.

Tramacere, Antonella. "Mirror Neurons in the Tree of Life, Development and Evolution of Sensorimotor Matching Responses." *Undefined*, 2016, www.semanticscholar.org/paper/Mirror-neurons-in-the-tree-of-life%2C-development-and-Tramacere/d3b10fba44f7a205f614e1a67aedf20602303252. Accessed 17 Jan. 2022.

The Thinker is a Shrinker

BalterJul. 25, Michael, et al. "The Incredible Shrinking Human Brain." *Science | AAAS*, 25 July 2011, www.sciencemag.org/news/2011/07/incredible-shrinking-human-brain.

Caspi, Yaron, et al. "Changes in the Intracranial Volume from Early Adulthood to the Sixth Decade of Life: A Longitudinal Study." *NeuroImage*, Apr. 2020, p. 116842, 10.1016/j.neuroimage.2020.116842. Accessed 16 June 2020.

Hare, Brian. "Survival of the Friendliest:Homo SapiensEvolved via Selection for Prosociality." *Annual Review of Psychology*, vol. 68, no. 1, 3 Jan. 2017, pp. 155–186, 10.1146/annurev-psych-010416-044201.

Huelke, Donald F. "An Overview of Anatomical Considerations of Infants and Children in the Adult World of Automobile Safety Design." *Annual Proceedings / Association for the Advancement of Automotive Medicine*, vol. 42, 1998, pp. 93–113, www.ncbi.nlm.nih.gov/pmc/articles/PMC3400202/.

Peters, R. "Ageing and the Brain." *Postgraduate Medical Journal*, vol. 82, no. 964, 1 Feb. 2006, pp. 84–88, www.ncbi.nlm.nih.gov/pmc/articles/PMC2596698/, 10.1136/pgmj.2005.036665.

Sherwood, Chet C., et al. "Aging of the Cerebral Cortex Differs between Humans and Chimpanzees." *Proceedings of the National Academy of Sciences*, vol. 108, no. 32, 25 July 2011, pp. 13029–13034, 10.1073/pnas.1016709108. Accessed 2 Apr. 2019.

"The Human Brain Has Been Getting Smaller since the Stone Age." *Discover Magazine*, www.discovermagazine.com/planet-earth/the-human-brain-has-been-getting-smaller-since-the-stone-age.

"The Truth about Aging and Dementia." *Centers for Disease Control and Prevention*, 2019, www.cdc.gov/aging/publications/features/dementia-not-normal-aging.html.

You Stem from Stem Cells

Aly, Riham Mohamed. "Current State of Stem Cell-Based Therapies: An Overview." *Stem Cell Investigation*, vol. 7, May 2020, pp. 8–8, 10.21037/sci-2020-001.

Boston Children's Hospital. "Where Do We Get Adult Stem Cells? «Boston Children's Hospital." *Childrenshospital.org*, 2009, stemcell.childrenshospital.org/about-stem-cells/adult-somatic-stem-cells-101/where-do-we-get-adult-stem-cells/.

"Frequently Asked Questions about Stem Cell Research." *Mayo Clinic*, www.mayoclinic.org/tests-procedures/bone-marrow-transplant/in-depth/stem-cells/art-20048117#:~:text=These%20stem%20cells%20are%20found.

Harvard Health Publishing. "Repairing the Heart with Stem Cells - Harvard Health." *Harvard Health*, Harvard Health, Mar. 2013, www.health.harvard.edu/heart-health/repairing-the-heart-with-stem-cells.

Masatani, Melissa. "Experimental Stem Cell Therapy Helps Paralyzed Man Regain Use of Arms and Hands." *HSC News*, hscnews.usc.edu/experimental-stem-cell-therapy-helps-paralyzed-man-regain-use-of-arms-and-hands.

Stanford Children's Health. "Stanford Children's Health." *Stanfordchildrens.org*, 2019, www.stanfordchildrens.org/en/topic/default?id=what-are-stem-cells-160-38.

"The Promise of Induced Pluripotent Stem Cells (IPSCs) | Stemcells.nih.gov." *Nih.gov*, 2000, stemcells.nih.gov/info/Regenerative_Medicine/2006chapter10.htm.

University of Nebraska Medical Center. "Types of Stem Cell | Stem Cells | University of Nebraska Medical Center." *Unmc.edu*, 2018, www.unmc.edu/stemcells/educational-resources/types.html.

"What Is the Difference between Totipotent, Pluripotent, and Multipotent? | NYSTEM." *Ny.gov*, 2020, stemcell.ny.gov/faqs/what-difference-between-totipotent-pluripotent-and-multipotent#:~:text=Pluripotent%20cells%20can%20give%20rise.

Reduce, Reuse, Recycle

Garber, Megan. "The Trash We've Left on the Moon." *The Atlantic*, 19 Dec. 2012, www.theatlantic.com/technology/archive/2012/12/the-trash-weve-left-on-the-moon/266465/.

"Human Urine Bricks Invented by South African Students." *BBC News*, 25 Oct. 2018, www.bbc.com/news/world-africa-45978942.

"Your Kidneys & How They Work | NIDDK." *National Institute of Diabetes and Digestive and Kidney Diseases*, www.niddk.nih.gov/health-information/kidney-disease/kidneys-how-they-work#:~:text=Your%20blood%20circulates%20through%20your. Accessed 17 Jan. 2022.

A Nifty Trip from Crypt to Tip

"Crypt to Tip: Migrating Gut Cells Adapt to Their Locations - Weizmann Wonder Wander - News, Features and Discoveries." *Weizmann Wonder Wander - News, Features and Discoveries from the Weizmann Institute of Science*, 22 Nov. 2018, wis-wander.weizmann.ac.il/life-sciences/crypt-tip-migrating-gut-cells-adapt-their-locations. Accessed 17 Jan. 2022.

"Life Cycle of Small Intestinal Enterocytes." *Colostate.edu*, 2018, www.vivo.colostate.edu/hbooks/pathphys/digestion/smallgut/lifecycle.html.

The Editors of Encyclopedia Britannica. "Villus | Anatomy." *Encyclopædia Britannica*, 27 June 2018, www.britannica.com/science/villus.

Human Print Queue

Agarwal, Swarnima, et al. "Current Developments in 3D Bioprinting for Tissue and Organ Regeneration—a Review." *Frontiers in Mechanical Engineering*, vol. 6, 30 Oct. 2020, 10.3389/fmech.2020.589171. Accessed 23 Nov. 2020.

Ma, Xuanyi, et al. "3D Bioprinting of Functional Tissue Models for Personalized Drug Screening and in Vitro Disease Modeling." *Advanced Drug Delivery Reviews*, vol. 132, July 2018, pp. 235–251, 10.1016/j.addr.2018.06.011.

Endo? Exo? Who Crine Figure this Out?

"Exocrine Gland | Physiology." *Encyclopedia Britannica*, www.britannica.com/science/exocrine-gland.

"Pituitary Gland." *www.hopkinsmedicine.org*, www.hopkinsmedicine.org/health/conditions-and-diseases/the-pituitary-gland#:~:text=The%20pituitary%20gland%20is%20sometimes.

Schwartz, Theodore B, and David O Norris. "Endocrine System | Anatomy." *Encyclopædia Britannica*, 17 Apr. 2019, www.britannica.com/science/endocrine-system.

Keep the Beat

"Just in Time Medicine." *www.justintimemedicine.com*, www.justintimemedicine.com/CurriculumContent/p/2306.

"NOVA Online | Cut to the Heart | Map of the Human Heart | Amazing Heart Facts." *www.pbs.org*, www.pbs.org/wgbh/nova/heart/heartfacts.html.

"Secrets of the Coupled Clock behind the Heart's Natural Pacemaker Cells." *National Institute on Aging*, www.nia.nih.gov/news/secrets-coupled-clock-behind-hearts-natural-pacemaker-cells.

Peculiar Platelets

Daly, Martina E. "Determinants of Platelet Count in Humans." *Haematologica*, vol. 96, no. 1, 1 Jan. 2011, pp. 10–13, www.ncbi.nlm.nih.gov/pmc/articles/PMC3012758/, 10.3324/haematol.2010.035287.

Garraud, Olivier, and Fabrice Cognasse. "Are Platelets Cells? And If Yes, Are They Immune Cells?" *Frontiers in Immunology*, vol. 6, 20 Feb. 2015, p. 70, www.ncbi.nlm.nih.gov/pmc/articles/PMC4335469/, 10.3389/fimmu.2015.00070. Accessed 30 Nov. 2021.

Patel, S. R. "The Biogenesis of Platelets from Megakaryocyte Proplatelets." *Journal of Clinical Investigation*, vol. 115, no. 12, 1 Dec. 2005, pp. 3348–3354, 10.1172/jci26891.

"Platelet Disorders." *Medlineplus.gov*, National Library of Medicine, 2019, medlineplus.gov/plateletdisorders.html.

"What Are Platelets?" *Stanfordchildrens.org*, 2020, www.stanfordchildrens.org/en/topic/default?id=what-are-platelets-160-36.

Williams, Marlene. "What Are Platelets and Why Are They Important?" *www.hopkinsmedicine.org*, 2021, www.hopkinsmedicine.org/health/conditions-and-diseases/what-are-platelets-and-why-are-they-important.

Lymph is No Wimp

Bradford, Alina. "Thymus: Facts, Function & Diseases." *Live Science*, Live Science, 10 May 2018, www.livescience.com/62527-thymus.html.

Cleveland Clinic. "Lymphatic System: Parts & Common Problems." *Cleveland Clinic*, 23 Feb. 2020, my.clevelandclinic.org/health/articles/21199-lymphatic-system.

Kim Ann Zimmermann. "Lymphatic System: Facts, Functions & Diseases." *Live Science*, Live Science, 21 Feb. 2018, www.livescience.com/26983-lymphatic-system.html.

"Overview of the Lymphatic System - Heart and Blood Vessel Disorders." *Merck Manuals Consumer Version*, www.merckmanuals.com/home/heart-and-blood-vessel-disorders/lymphatic-disorders/overview-of-the-lymphatic-system#:~:text=Most%20of%20the%20lymphatic%20vessels. Accessed 17 Jan. 2022.

"Spleen | SEER Training." *Training.seer.cancer.gov*, training.seer.cancer.gov/anatomy/lymphatic/components/spleen.html.

"Thymus | Gland | Britannica." *Encyclopædia Britannica*, 2019, www.britannica.com/science/thymus.

Call in the (Immuno)Cavalry

"How Immunotherapy Is Used to Treat Cancer." *Cancer.org*, American Cancer Society, 2015, www.cancer.org/treatment/treatments-and-side-effects/treatment-types/immunotherapy/what-is-immunotherapy.html.

"How Tumor Cells Evade the Immune Defense: Study Led by the University of Bonn Might Help to Improve Modern Therapeutic Approaches." *ScienceDaily*, www.sciencedaily.com/releases/2020/08/200805102038.htm.

"Immunotherapy." *www.lls.org*, 26 Feb. 2015, www.lls.org/treatment/types-of-treatment/immunotherapy.

National Cancer Institute. "NCI Dictionary of Cancer Terms." *National Cancer Institute*, 2 Feb. 2011, www.cancer.gov/publications/dictionaries/cancer-terms/def/immune-check-point-inhibitor.

"What Is Immunotherapy for Cancer? - Dana-Farber Cancer Institute | Boston, MA." *www.dana-Farber.org*, www.dana-farber.org/health-library/articles/what-is-immunotherapy-for-cancer-/.

"What Is Immunotherapy?" *Cancer Research Institute*, 2018, www.cancerresearch.org/immunotherapy/what-is-immunotherapy.

Fight Back with a Vac(cine)

British Society for Immunology. "How Vaccines Work | British Society for Immunology." *www.immunology.org*, 2020, www.immunology.org/celebrate-vaccines/public-engagement/guide-childhood-vaccinations/how-vaccines-work.

"Innate and Adaptive Immunity - American Society for Radiation Oncology (ASTRO) - American Society for Radiation Oncology (ASTRO)." *ASTRO*, 2016, www.astro.org/Patient-Care-and-Research/Research/Professional-Development/Research-Primers/Innate-and-Adaptive-Immunity.

Institute for Quality and Efficiency in Health Care. "The Innate and Adaptive Immune Systems." *Nih.gov*, Institute for Quality and Efficiency in Health Care (IQWiG), 30 July 2020, www.ncbi.nlm.nih.gov/books/NBK279396/.

Pappas, Stephanie. "How Do Vaccines Work?" *Live Science*, Live Science, June 2010, www.livescience.com/32617-how-do-vaccines-work.html.

U.S. Department of Health & Human Services. "Vaccine Types | Vaccines." *Vaccines.gov*, 2017, www.vaccines.gov/basics/types.

World Health Organization. "How Do Vaccines Work?" *www.who.int*, WHO, 8 Dec. 2020, www.who.int/news-room/feature-stories/detail/how-do-vaccines-work.

What You Want, or What You Needle?

Kulick, Lisa. "An Alternative to the Syringe." *Engineering.cmu.edu*, engineering.cmu.edu/news-events/news/2020/04/07-microneedle-array.html.

"Microscopic STAR Particles Offer New Potential Treatment for Skin Diseases | News Center." *News.gatech.edu*, news.gatech.edu/2020/03/09/microscopic-star-particles-offer-new-potential-treatment-skin-diseases. Accessed 17 Jan. 2022.

Tadros, Andrew R., et al. "STAR Particles for Enhanced Topical Drug and Vaccine Delivery." *Nature Medicine*, vol. 26, no. 3, 1 Mar. 2020, pp. 341–347, pubmed.ncbi.nlm.nih.gov/32152581/, 10.1038/s41591-020-0787-6. Accessed 17 Jan. 2022.

Yang, Jian, et al. "Recent Advances of Microneedles for Biomedical Applications: Drug Delivery and Beyond." *Acta Pharmaceutica Sinica B*, vol. 9, no. 3, May 2019, pp. 469–483, www.sciencedirect.com/science/article/pii/S2211383518312437, 10.1016/j.apsb.2019.03.007.

"Big Eaters", Big Appetites

"Macrophage | Ask a Biologist." *Asu.edu*, 14 Feb. 2011, askabiologist.asu.edu/macrophage.

"Macrophages: The 'Defense' Cells That Help throughout the Body." *ScienceDaily*, 2010, www.sciencedaily.com/releases/2010/08/100826141232.htm.

Saldana, José Ignacio. "Macrophages | British Society for Immunology." *Immunology.org*, 2016, www.immunology.org/public-information/bitesized-immunology/cells/macrophages.

Eye Need Some Lasers

Clinkc, Wolfe Eye. "LASIK Surgery & Recovery Process | Wolfe Eye Clinic." *www.wolfeeyeclinic.com*, www.wolfeeyeclinic.com/lasik/lasik-surgery-and-technology. Accessed 17 Jan. 2022.

Mayo Clinic. "LASIK Eye Surgery - Mayo Clinic." *Mayoclinic.org*, 8 Nov. 2019, www.mayoclinic.org/tests-procedures/lasik-eye-surgery/about/pac-20384774.

"What Is 20/20 Vision?" *University of Iowa Hospitals & Clinics*, 2 July 2016, uihc.org/health-topics/what-2020-vision#:~:text=Only%20about%2035%20percent%20of.

ABOUT THE AUTHORS

Jenn and Charlie are Boston-based science nerds who met through stand-up comedy. By day, Jenn writes science textbooks and Charlie slings data for a lab in a cancer research hospital. By night, they make comedy films and dream about starting a new TikTok dance craze called The Microbe Mash.